WATCHMEN WHO WOULDN'T QUIT

PAM & STAN CAMPBELL

WATCHMEN WHO WOULDN'T QUIT

A DIVISION OF SCRIPTURE PRESS PUBLICATIONS INC.
USA CANADA ENGLAND

BibleLog Thru the Old Testament Series
Book 1   **Let There Be Life** (Genesis thru Ruth)
Book 2   **Who's Running This Kingdom?** (1 Samuel thru 2 Chronicles)
Book 3   **Tunes, Tales, and Truths** (Ezra thru Song of Songs)
Book 4   **Watchmen Who Wouldn't Quit** (Isaiah thru Malachi)

BibleLog Thru the New Testament Series
Book 1   **When God Left Footprints** (Matthew thru John)
Book 2   **Good News to Go** (Acts thru 1 Corinthians)
Book 3   **Priority Mail** (2 Corinthians thru Philemon)
Book 4   **Home At Last** (Hebrews thru Revelation)

BibleLog for Adults is an inductive Bible study series designed to take you through the Bible in 2 years if you study one session each week. This eight-book series correlates with SonPower's **BibleLog** series for youth. You may want to use **BibleLog** in your daily quiet time, completing a chapter a week by working through a few pages each day. Or you may want to use this series (along with the SonPower **BibleLog** series) in family devotions with your teenagers. This book also includes a leader's guide for use in small groups.

Scripture taken from the *Holy Bible, New International Version* ®. Copyright © 1973, 1978, 1984 by International Bible Society. Used by permission of Zondervan Publishing House. All rights reserved.

Designer: Joe DeLeon
Cover Illustration: Jeff Nishinaka
Interior Illustrations: Arnie Ten

Library of Congress Catalog Card Number: 92-082619
ISBN: 0-89693-874-3

Recommended Dewey Decimal Classification: 224.5
Suggested Subject Heading: BIBLE STUDY: PROPHETIC BOOKS

1 2 3 4 5 6 7 8 9 10 Printing/Year 96 95 94 93 92

© 1992, SP Publications, Inc.
All rights reserved.
Printed in the United States of America.

CONTENTS

BEFORE YOU BEGIN 6
FROM THE AUTHORS 9
  1. Any Volunteers? 11
  2. Bright Hope for Tomorrow 25
  3. It's Lonely at the Bottom 37
  4. The Negative Effects of Tell-a-Vision 49
  5. Out of This World 61
  6. Who's Responsible Here? 73
  7. When the Heat Is On 87
  8. Out of the Future, into the Lions' Den 99
  9. Lousy Is Thy Faithfulness 111
  10. Unsafe and Secure 125
  11. What's Your Verdict? 137
  12. What Do You Expect? 149
BEFORE YOU LEAVE 161

LEADER'S GUIDE 163
  Session 1 165
  Session 2 166
  Session 3 167
  Session 4 168
  Session 5 169
  Session 6 170
  Session 7 171
  Session 8 172
  Session 9 173
  Session 10 174
  Session 11 175
  Session 12 176
  Review 177
  Prophet Trivia 178

WRAP-UP 179

BEFORE YOU BEGIN

Welcome to Book 4 in the
BibleLog Thru the Old Testament Series

Though the Bible continues to be one of the world's best-selling books, few people are familiar enough with it to comprehend "the big picture." They may know many of the specific stories about Abraham, Samson, Jonah, Jesus, Peter, Paul, and so forth. Yet most people are unsure how these characters fit into the broad historic groupings—patriarchs, judges, kings, prophets, Gospels, epistles, etc.

That's why we are introducing the **BibleLog Thru the Old Testament Series.** The purpose of the **BibleLog** studies is to guide you through the Old Testament in one year, at the rate of one session per week. This series eliminates the perceived drudgery of Bible reading by removing unnecessary references and explaining the material in clear terms that anyone can understand. The pace should be fast enough to propel you through the material without getting bogged down, yet slow enough to allow you to see things you never noticed before. First-time readers will feel completely at ease as they explore the Bible on their own. Yet no matter how many times the person has been through the Bible, this study will provide fresh insight.

WHAT MAKES BIBLELOG DIFFERENT?
Countless thousands of adults have, at some point in their lives, decided to read through the Bible. Pastors, Sunday School teachers, Bible study leaders, or peers have preached the benefits of "Read your Bible," "Get into the Word," "Meditate on Scripture," and so forth. And after hearing so many worthwhile challenges, a lot of determined, committed adults have dusted off the covers of their Bibles and set themselves to the task ahead.

They usually make a noble effort too. The first couple of Bible books whiz past before they know it. The next few books aren't quite as fast-paced, but they have their strong points. Then comes a tough passage. In most cases, the Gospels are enough to do in even the most eager readers. And instead of feeling like they've accomplished something, all those people feel is guilt because they didn't finish what they started.

That's why this Bible study series was developed. It calls for a one-year commitment on your part to get through the Old Testament. By following the session plans provided, you only need to complete one session each week to accomplish your one-year goal. You won't read the entire Old Testament word for word, but you will go much more in-depth than most of the Old Testament overviews you may have tried. You will still be challenged just to get through the major flow of Old Testament action in one year.

WHAT ARE THE FEATURES OF BIBLELOG?

- **THE WHOLE BIBLE** Not a verse-by-verse study, but an approach that hits all the books without skipping major passages.

- **THE RIGHT PACE** By completing one session each week (a couple of pages per day), you will get through the Old Testament in one year.

- **A FRESH APPROACH** The inductive design allows you to personally interact with biblical truth. Longer, drier passages are summarized in the text, and difficult passages are explained, but you are kept involved in the discovery process at all times.

- **INSTANT APPLICATION** Each weekly session concludes with a **Journey Inward** section of practical application that allows you to respond to the content immediately. The goal is to help you apply the truths of the Bible today.

- **GROUP STUDY OPTION** A leader's guide is included to promote discussion and further application if desired. After a week of self-study, a time of group interaction can be very effective in reinforcing God's truth. Each book covers 13 weeks.

- **REASONABLE PRICE** The entire set of 4 Old Testament **BibleLog** books costs no more than a basic Bible commentary. And after completing the series, you will have a self-written commentary of the Old Testament for future reference.

- **48 DIFFERENT TOPICS** Over a one-year period of study, you will be challenged to apply what the Bible has to say about 48 different topics, including God's sovereignty, murder, homosexuality, obedience, family relationships, and much more.

HOW CAN YOU GET THE MOST OUT OF BIBLELOG?

We recommend a group study for this series, if possible. If group members work through the content of the sessions individually during the week, the time your group needs to spend going over facts will be greatly reduced. With the content portion completed prior to the group meeting, your group time can emphasize the application of the biblical concepts to your individual members. A leader's guide is included at the back of the book to direct you in a review of the content. But the real strength of the leader's guide is to show you how to apply what you are learning. If you don't have the opportunity to go through this series with a group, that's OK too. Just be sure to think through all of the **Journey Inward** sections at the end of each session.

FROM THE AUTHORS

Welcome to Book 4 of the **BibleLog** Series. This book is titled *Watchmen Who Wouldn't Quit* because it covers the prophetic books of the Old Testament. Recognizing how little most people know about the prophets, you probably aren't jumping up and down shouting, "Oh goody, goody! At last I get to do some serious study on all those guys with the funny names!"

Perhaps you're even being "challenged" to do this study against your will. When you begin to approach the prophetic books, suddenly all those other studies on love and sex, knowing God's will, peer pressure, discipleship, and so forth, seem more appealing. While the prophetic books may be a little more dry and repetitive than, say, Song of Songs, it's fair to say that they are also beneficial and dynamic. In fact, the prophets will bring you a lot of solid help in the areas of love and sex, knowing God's will, peer pressure, discipleship, and much more.

You may have another reason to resist a study of the prophets. When you take the pages of all the books between Isaiah and Malachi and put them between your thumb and forefinger, you'll find that you're holding a big hunk of the Bible. Don't let that concern you, though. The 12 sessions in this book take the same amount of effort as any of the previous ones in the **BibleLog** Series. (Just don't be surprised if you find yourself wanting to go back and spend more time with several of the passages you'll be going through so quickly.)

The prophets were a terrific bunch of men, and they deserve a lot more attention than they usually get. Try to get to know them as people as you try to understand all they have to say. It doesn't take a prophet to predict that you won't be disappointed.

Pam and Stan Campbell

You're pretty good at expressing your thoughts on paper, but to speak to hundreds of parents—you're not sure you can do it.

1
ANY VOLUNTEERS?
(Isaiah 1—39)

The score is tied. It's late in the fourth quarter of the gridiron battle, as the Hometown Hopefuls go up against the Midtown Manglers. And things look grim for the Hometown team. No one has been able to stop Midtown's linebacker, "Crusher" Cranston. Crusher has already taken out two—oops, make that three—of our best players. And as the Coach looks up and down his empty bench, there's only one player left now to put in. You! And to be truthful, you've never been a hall-of-fame quality player. Much less against meat-grinders like Crusher Cranston. So are you up to the task?

· ·

You've never spoken in public before. Shucks, you get nervous when you have to place your order in a restaurant. But you've been invited to be the plenary speaker at the annual meeting of the PTA. Sure, you had some good ideas of how parents could be more supportive of authority figures, and you're pretty good at expressing your thoughts on paper. But to stand in front of dozens—no, make that hundreds—of parents—you're not sure you can do it. What do you think?

· ·

What other situations do you face where it's hard for you to gather your courage and do something that's really hard for you to do? Think of as many examples as you can, and write them below.

 **JOURNEY ONWARD**

In this book, we're going to take a look at the Old Testament prophets and their writings. We especially want to observe the prophets themselves, because they were a special group of people. You may not know too much about the prophets. (Most people don't.) But you probably do know that these guys were the ones who often stood alone and proclaimed God's message to mass quantities of people who didn't particularly want to hear what God (or the prophet) had to say.

And one of the first questions we should ask ourselves is: What kind of personality would it take to be a prophet? Wouldn't you have to have an above average self-image and tons of confidence? Or would you just have to be a little crazy? Or both?

It won't take you too long to find out that many of the prophets were people not unlike yourself. You'll discover that some of these guys had deep personal problems (for instance, a wife who fooled around with other men). Some were terrified to do what God told them, and even ran the opposite direction. (That's right—Jonah.) And many of the others were just ordinary people who felt overwhelmed to be chosen by God to deliver His messages. They didn't start out as "spiritual giants." But they allowed God to use them, and they became heroes in their own right. You'll see that for yourself as you examine the first prophet on the list—Isaiah.

Isaiah's name means, "The Lord saves," and that was also his basic message to the people. He lived during the period when Israel was growing weaker (spiritually) and when the Assyrians were growing stronger (militaristically). You should remember from *Who's Running This Kingdom?* (Book 2 of the

Any Volunteers?

BibleLog series) that the Assyrians eventually conquered Israel and carried them off into captivity. Isaiah was aware of what was going to happen ahead of time. You'll see that he prophesied judgment and bad times ahead for Israel, but he also promised them better times to come. As a personal note, Isaiah was married and had a couple of kids.

Read Isaiah 1:1-31.
Which kings of Israel reigned during Isaiah's years of prophesying? (Isaiah 1:1)

How can you tell that God was displeased with Israel at this point in its history? (1:2-4, 8-9)

Getting Personal — *How do you know when God is displeased with you?*

The Israelites hadn't stopped offering sacrifices to God. In fact, God said that He had "more than enough of burnt offerings" (1:11). So why was God angry with His people? (1:10-15)

What did God want Israel to do? (1:16-17)

What promise did He make to Israel? (1:18-20)

Watchmen Who Wouldn't Quit

Read Isaiah 2:1-22.
Isaiah knew God's judgment was going to come upon Israel. But he also saw beyond the punishment. What did he see in store for Israel "in the last days"? (2:1-5)

What specific complaint did God have against Israel at this time? (2:6-9)

When God gets around to dealing with His people, what will happen to their "precious" idols? (2:20)

Read Isaiah 3:1–4:6.
Israel and Judah were sinful, but the thing that really intensified God's anger toward them was that they were also proud. They had no concern or remorse regarding their sin (3:8-9). But their pride was going to come to an end. Summarize the before-and-after picture that Isaiah described (3:16–4:1).

Read Isaiah 5:1-30.
Read Isaiah's parable in 5:1-7. List the main images in the parable and what you think each image symbolizes.

Read Isaiah 6:1-13.
You can see the state to which the nation of Israel had sunk. It is in that context that Isaiah was called to speak for God. He had a vision of being in God's presence. What specific things did Isaiah see in his vision? (6:1-4)

Any Volunteers?

How did Isaiah feel in the presence of God? (6:5)

What happened to Isaiah to change his attitude? (6:6-7)

Exactly how did his attitude change? (6:8)

What assignment did God give Isaiah? (6:9-13)

Getting Personal — *What task do you think God has for you?*

Read Isaiah 7:1-25.
Isaiah's vision of God took place in the last year of the life of King Uzziah. Later, during the reign of King Ahaz, God sent another important message through Isaiah. But Ahaz didn't want to receive a sign from God (7:10-13), so Isaiah told of the sign that God would send to remind people of His presence on earth. What would it be? (7:14)

[NOTE: "Immanuel" means "God is with us."]

Isaiah's prophecy to Ahaz was probably twofold. First, God was trying to tell the king that in the near future, God would be with him to help deliver him from his enemies, the Assyrians (7:15-25). And then, of course, someday the

Son of God Himself would come to earth to deliver us from another enemy, Satan.

Read Isaiah 8:1-22.
Isaiah 8 contains another significant passage to help us understand the nature of God. According to Isaiah, God can be either a "sanctuary" or "a stone that causes men to stumble and a rock that makes them fall" (v. 14). What determines which side of God's nature people see? (8:11-17)

Light in Darkness
Read Isaiah 9:1-21.
Isaiah knew that Israel was in spiritual darkness, but he also knew that a light would be coming. Review 9:1-7. Who or what do you think that light is? What makes you think so?

Make a special note of the names used to describe the coming "light" (9:6). What positive qualities would you expect each of the following titles to indicate?

❏ Wonderful Counselor

❏ Mighty God

❏ Everlasting Father

Any Volunteers?

❑ Prince of Peace

Skim Isaiah 10:1–11:16.
Soon after, Isaiah made a similar prophecy: the coming of a leader who will be from the house of Jesse. (Jesse, you should remember, was the father of King David.) God had promised David, "Your house and your kingdom will endure forever before Me; your throne will be established forever" (2 Samuel 7:16). God's message to David supports Isaiah's prophecies concerning the coming of Jesus.

But here's the problem: David's kingdom (Israel and Judah) apparently came to an end *before* Jesus came to earth. When Israel, and then Judah, were carried into captivity, there were no more kings. And we know that Jesus wasn't born into a royal household. So how does Isaiah illustrate the gap between the last kings of Judah and the kingdom that Jesus establishes? (Isaiah 11:1)

What kind of person will the "Branch" be? (11:2-5)

When the Branch's kingdom is fully realized, how will life on earth be different than it is now? (11:6-9)

Skim Isaiah 12:1–14:32.
Another familiar portion of Isaiah is in chapter 14. Verses 12-17 (and following) describe the fall of the "morning star," which can also be translated "Lucifer." Many people understand this to be a description of Satan's fall from heaven. Others don't. But in either case, the passage was an

address to the king of Babylon (14:3) and deserves notice for what it teaches concerning pride.

Isaiah had already explained that God would have compassion on Israel (14:1) and would step in to give His people relief from their bondage (14:3-4). What visual image did Isaiah use to describe the leader of Babylon then? (14:12)

What attitude did this guy have? (14:13-14)

What end was in store for this wicked leader? (14:15-20)

Skim Isaiah 15:1–35:10.
Babylon wasn't to be the only empire to suffer because of its sinful ways. In the next several chapters of Isaiah, the prophet forecast bad times ahead for a number of evil places—including Assyria, the land of the Philistines, Moab, Damascus, Cush, Egypt, Edom, Arabia, and Tyre. Isaiah even prophesied a dim future for the earth as a whole to look forward to (Isaiah 24, especially vv. 19-23). Even Jerusalem, at one time David's glorious city, was to be subject to God's judgment. What did Isaiah predict about the future of Jerusalem? (22:1-4)

What was the attitude of the Israelites toward God and His messengers, the prophets? (30:8-11)

Any Volunteers?

Assyria at the Gate
Read Isaiah 36:1-22.
Yet before God allowed the people of Judah to go into captivity, He showed them what He could do for them—if they would put their trust in Him, that is. The Assyrian army, led by a man named Sennacherib, surrounded Jerusalem (36:1). Hezekiah was the king of Judah at that time, so several of his people went out to meet with some of the Assyrian leaders. The Assyrians sent a message to Hezekiah. What did they want him to do? (36:8)

Hezekiah's assistants wanted the Assyrian delegation to speak in Aramaic—a language that *they* could understand, but that couldn't be interpreted by the people inside the city who might happen to overhear (36:11). But the Assyrians *wanted* the people inside to hear, so they shouted out in Hebrew. What did the Assyrians tell the people of Judah? (36:11-21)

Read Isaiah 37:1-38.
When King Hezekiah received this report, what did he do? (37:1-4)

What advice did Isaiah give Hezekiah? (37:5-7)

In the meantime, Sennacherib sent another threatening message to Hezekiah (37:9-13). What did Hezekiah do in response this time? (37:14-15)

19

What did Isaiah have to say? (37:21-23, 29, 33-35)

How were Isaiah's words fulfilled? (37:36-37)

What happened to the "mighty" Sennacherib? (37:38)

If this story sounds familiar to you, it's a repeat of one of the accounts you may have studied in *Who's Running This Kingdom?* (Book 2 of the **BibleLog** series). But it's a good one to repeat, especially here in relation to Isaiah's ministry.

Read Isaiah 38:1-22.
There's another story repeated here in case you've forgotten what makes Hezekiah a distinctive king. If you remember what made King Hezekiah's last years so special, write down what you can recall. If you're drawing a blank, review the facts in Isaiah 38:1-7 and summarize them below. (Then go back to 2 Kings 20:1-11 to jog your memory about your first contact with Isaiah and King Hezekiah.)

Read Isaiah 39:1-8.
One final story of Hezekiah is repeated in the Book of Isaiah. After Hezekiah's terrific experience with the positive power of prayer, he used some really bad judgment late in his life. What did he do? (39:1-2)

Any Volunteers?

Getting Personal – *When was the last time you used bad judgment?*

Hezekiah's bad judgment prompted another prophecy by Isaiah. What did the prophet say was going to happen? (39:3-7)

 JOURNEY INWARD

The message of this session seems to swing like a pendulum. First there's a description of the horrible spiritual state of Israel and Judah. Then Isaiah is allowed to see the holiness and glory of God. Several passages refer to the sure-to-come captivity of God's people, yet others look beyond that point to a time when God will establish His kingdom the way it *should* be. And all of these passages, when compared and contrasted, can provide some real insight into the area of **confidence**.

Confidence means different things to different people. Lots of people think of confidence as self-assurance, or the ability to handle any crisis with their own talents and powers. Others seem to think of confidence as optimism—the unsubstantiated belief that problems will somehow resolve themselves. (These people have no good reasons to believe such a thing, but their everything-is-going-to-get-better attitude seems to get them through some tough spots.)

Isaiah, as you have seen, was a confident person. But he was too smart to think that things would get better on their own. (He saw exactly what rotten shape his world was in.) And he had no confidence in his own ability: when he saw the desperate condition of the people, his first response was, "Woe is me" (6:5). He knew he was just one more sinful person in a nation full of them.

So what was it that made Isaiah so confident? Simple. He allowed God to forgive his sins and cleanse him. After the angel touched his lips with the live coal from the altar, Isaiah's attitude changed from, "Woe is me," to, "Here am I.

21

Send me!" Isaiah's confidence was based on his belief that God could handle any problem that came up. A nation full of sinful people? God was in control of all the nations, and could lead His people to repentance. Threats from nasty armies? No problem. God could immediately eliminate 185,000 soldiers and cause the rest of them to turn around and go home. And after realizing what God was capable of doing, Isaiah became *confident*.

To help you determine how confident *you* are, answer the following questions:

❑ What do you depend on when you're really afraid?

❑ Do you ever dare to stand alone for your beliefs, even against tremendous opposition? (Give specific examples.)

❑ Do you *really* expect (and receive) results from prayer?

❑ Have you ever compromised on a big issue and then been sorry about it later on?

You know how Isaiah would have answered each of these questions. If *your* answers aren't what you know they *should* be, then maybe you need to stop counting on yourself so much and depend on God more. Confidence is more than just self-talk. ("I can do anything. I'm smart and strong. There's nothing too tough for me.") Confidence is resting in the certainty that *God* can do anything and everything.

Any Volunteers?

To close, think of the areas in your life where you need more confidence (making new friends, talking to others about God, saying no to things you know to be wrong, etc.). Write them all below.

Now spend some time asking God for the confidence to succeed in each of the areas you have listed. Remember to confess any sins you can think of and to make sure God is the source of your confidence. Then you'll really see a difference in the quality of your life. You can be confident of it.

**KEY VERSE**
"If you do not stand firm in your faith, you will not stand at all" (Isaiah 7:9).

23

When you have a major presentation coming up at work the next day, do you briefly prepare and hope for the best?

2
BRIGHT HOPE FOR TOMORROW
(Isaiah 40—66)

When you have a major presentation coming up at work the next day and you aren't really prepared for it, what do you do?

- ❏ Conduct an all-night session to slap something together.
- ❏ Spend hours inventing a creative, never-before-heard excuse and explain to your understanding supervisor that you need more time.
- ❏ Record all the necessary information for your presentation on a tape loop and play it over and over and over again while you sleep.
- ❏ Work a couple of hours the night before and then just hope you can remember everything the next day.

When you're desperate for a date with the new person in your singles' group, what do you do?

- ❏ Plan to "accidentally" run into that person at your next meeting.
- ❏ Send the person a card, signed "from your secret admirer," and *then* run into the person a dozen times until you are noticed.
- ❏ Arrange for your friends to talk to his (or her) friends so that they can tell them that you are interested in him (or her).
- ❏ Go about your business as usual and hope that the person notices you.

When you audition for community theater, what do you do until you discover whether or not you got the part?

- ❏ Set up a 24-hour stakeout around your telephone, beating off other family

members until someone calls to give you the news.
- ❏ Pace the floor until you wear out a three-inch-deep furrow in your carpet.
- ❏ Spread the word for all your friends to keep their ears open and let you know the second they hear something.
- ❏ Stick to your normal routine and hope that you got the part.

You may notice that the last choice for each question seems to be the option that requires the least amount of energy. Most of us have come to think of "hope" as something to do as a last resort. If you can't take a specific action to solve a problem, you may as well "hope for the best."

So when the Bible says, as it does in this week's key verse, to "hope in the Lord," it might seem like an unsure method for dealing with your troubles. But the concept of "hope" in a biblical sense is based on the *certainty* that God is there to help you out. So to "hope in the Lord" is to be confident that you are not alone with your problems, and that He will help you through them. Conversely, to "hope things work out" is based on nothing concrete, so it is little consolation during turbulent times.

This session should help you see that hope in the Lord is something you can sink all your trust in when you need support. The main reason that Christian hope sometimes seems feeble is that we don't place a high priority on it. In most cases, we plunge ahead in our own limited ability instead of doing the right thing—depending on God to act in our lives. So let's see how Isaiah learned to let his hope in God get him through some extremely difficult times.

 **JOURNEY ONWARD**

The subject of hope is prevalent in chapters 40–66 of the Book of Isaiah. You'll remember that much of the first 39 chapters had to do with God's judgment—of Israel and the countries that had caused Israel so many problems. Yet God wanted to assure His people that His judgment would definitely be followed by His forgiveness, His mercy, and His love.

Yes, God would allow His people to be taken into captivity for a while. But He also promised to lead them out and eventually provide them a home that would never fall at the hands of an enemy. So the theme of the Book of

Isaiah shifts from judgment to hope.

Read Isaiah 40:1-31.
What is the first message from God recorded in this section of the Book of Isaiah? (40:1-2)

Isaiah 40:3 is quoted in the New Testament in reference to John the Baptist (Matthew 3:1-3). God had told Isaiah to tell the people to prepare for something. What was it that John the Baptist would prepare them for? (Isaiah 40:3)

The Israelites had been ignoring God, so God provided some illustrations to show them the effects of what they were doing. What symbols did God use to describe people who ignored Him? (40:6-8, 15, 17)

Getting Personal — *Have you ever ignored God? If so, which symbol do you relate to the most?*

But when people trust in God, how does that affect His relationship with them? (40:11)

Even though the Israelites were forgetting that they were supposed to serve the everlasting God, Isaiah brought a message of hope and promise for those who turned to God. What promises did Isaiah make? (40:27-31)

Read Isaiah 41:1-20.
Even knowing that God's people were going to be temporarily overpowered by foreign armies, what other promise did Isaiah deliver from God? (41:10)

Isaiah then predicted that God would send a servant. What would that servant do? (42:1-4)

Now flash forward in your Bible to Matthew 12:15-21. How did Jesus fulfill this prophecy of Isaiah?

Read Isaiah 42:1-25.
But during this time in their history, the Israelites weren't ready to hear promises about the coming of one of God's special messengers. They didn't even respect what the prophets (like Isaiah) were saying to their faces. Even though they called themselves servants of God, what did God have to say about His "servants"? (Isaiah 42:18-20)

Idol Worship
Read Isaiah 41:21-29.
Idolatry was a major problem at this time, and Isaiah had as much to say about idols as any of the other prophets. He wanted the people to see idols for what they really were. And much of what he had to say was somewhat sarcastic. For example, he described a scene where God challenges the people to gather their idols and obtain wisdom about events of the past or what will happen in the future. What is the obvious outcome of such an effort? (41:21-24)

Getting Personal – *Do you have any "idols" in your life? What are they?*

Read Isaiah 43:1-28.
What is one bad thing that happened when the Israelites began to worship idols? (43:22-24)

Read Isaiah 44:12-20.
What, if anything, was special about the people who made the idols? (44:12)

What, if anything, was special about the materials from which idols were made? (44:13-19)

Read Isaiah 46:1-13.
How capable is an idol of supporting those who worship it? (46:6-7)

Read Isaiah 57:1-10.
How did idol worship influence the day-to-day lives and habits of the Israelites? (57:3-10)

How dependable were the idols that the Israelites worshiped? (40:19-20)

Do you see the picture of false gods that Isaiah painted for the people? He pointed out that a bunch of ordinary people gathered a bunch of ordinary wood and metal, and designed a "god." Then they need skilled craftsmen (or a large tube of Crazy Glue) to keep the thing from falling over. And then, of course, the idol was stuck there with no mobility of its own. Isaiah asked, "*This* is the thing you choose to worship? *This* is what you're putting your trust in? *This* is what you sacrifice your own children to?"

Read Isaiah 44:1-11, 21-28.
Through their idols, the people "hoped" everything would be OK for them. And as much as it stretched the imagination to believe that an idol could bring comfort, knowledge, and power to people, the Israelites were making an even greater mistake by what they were overlooking. What basic facts were God's people ignoring as they entered into idol worship? (44:6-8)

Read Isaiah 45:1-10.
To what did Isaiah compare the stubborn people of Israel? (45:9-10)

Getting Personal — *How stubborn would you rate yourself?*

Skim Isaiah 47:1–49:26.
Perhaps by now you're thinking that all this doesn't sound much like a message of hope and comfort. But before God could show His wayward people how much He loved them (by bringing them out of captivity), He first had to make it clear why He was going to allow them to be overpowered in the first place. God knew He was dealing with stubborn people (48:4-5). And Isaiah was specific in his description of what would happen to Israel and Judah. God *would* allow them to suffer (48:10-11), but He would deliver them as well (48:20). What illustration did God use to describe the concern

He had for His people? (49:14-15)

Read Isaiah 45:11-25.
Isaiah even named the person who would release the Israelites from captivity. Who was it? (45:13)

[If you don't remember anything about this person, review Ezra 1.]

Skim Isaiah 50:1–54:17.
Isaiah reminded the people of God's power (50:1-11), of Abraham and their history (51:1-2), and of God's promises to them (51–52). Then Isaiah again focused on the person whom God would eventually send to redeem His people. What kind of person was He to be? (53:1-3)

What would He do for humankind? (53:4-6)

What would happen to Him? (53:7-9)

After that, what would happen to Him? (53:10-12)

Read Isaiah 55:1-13.
What invitation would God give to His people when the exiles returned? (55:1-3)

Getting Personal – *How might the same invitation apply to people today?*

What other instructions and challenges are just as relevant today as they were for the Israelites during Isaiah's time? (55:6-9)

How effective and influential are God's words? (55:10-11)

Skim Isaiah 56:1-12; 57:11-21; 58:1-14.
Isaiah also called on the people to examine the purpose and the effects of their worship habits. It wasn't enough for them to forsake idols just so they could spend the same amount of time with God. At least, not if their "worship" was only a meaningless ritual to them. True worship was supposed to have meaning in their lives. So how did Isaiah challenge the Israelites to improve each of the following elements of worship:

❑ Fasting? (58:3-9a)

❑ Service/Obedience? (58:9b-12)

❑ Respecting the Sabbath? (58:13-14)

Skim Isaiah 59:1–66:24.
As Isaiah approached the end of his writings, he again went over the main points of his message. He said that sin had separated the Israelites from God, and as a result, they were going to lose their freedom (59:1-19). But God wasn't going to forget them, and He would return them to their homeland (60:1-17). And even better, God was planning good things for His people as well as judgment for Israel's enemies (60:18–65:16). The good things would

Bright Hope for Tomorrow

include their redemption (59:20), respect from surrounding countries (60:10-14), peace (60:18), everlasting life in an eternal city (60:19-22), joy (61:7), and new heavens and a new earth (65:17-25). And in the last chapter of the Book of Isaiah, the prophet was still contrasting the hope of the righteous with the judgment of the wicked. What final cause for hope did the prophet leave with the people? (66:1-2, 13)

 **JOURNEY INWARD**

As you have just seen, **hope** was a powerful motivator for Isaiah. It wasn't just a last resort. Since Isaiah was confident that he could put his hope in God, he didn't have to panic when he saw things falling apart around him. And did you notice *how* Isaiah was able to sustain such a high level of hope? He did two major things: (1) He made sure he obeyed God in everything he did, and (2) He looked beyond the immediate problem in order to see the ultimate solution.

The importance of the first point should be obvious. If hope is to be based on God's ability to see you through a tough spot, then disobedience (ignoring God's wishes) will separate you from your only genuine source of workable hope. The second point probably needs a little thought. God didn't spare Isaiah from seeing the immediate (grim) future. If Isaiah had only looked that far, the future may have seemed hopeless indeed. But God also showed Isaiah what would happen *after* the bad stuff. And as Isaiah became assured of Israel's eventual release from captivity, he discovered he had a solid reason to hold on to his hope in God.

We can take comfort in the fact that God allowed Isaiah to look into *our* futures. Isaiah foretold Jesus' first coming to earth, and everything he prophesied came true. So we have no reason to doubt the accuracy of Isaiah's prophecies about Jesus' second coming for the fulfillment of His kingdom and comfort of His people. The hope we have for the future is not in vain.

You may be facing a number of problems that diminish your hope for the future. If so, list them in the left-hand column on the following chart. Then

33

examine yourself and see if you are being disobedient to God in any way. In the second column, list any changes you might need to make. Then think of a biblical promise that applies to the problem(s) you listed and how that promise will affect the problem(s). In the third column, imagine the potential effects of that promise coming true in your life.

PROBLEMS	POSSIBLE SIN PROBLEMS	REASONS FOR HOPE

If you can't think of a promise to apply to your specific problems, don't give up. Use a Bible concordance for starters. (Check all the key words and synonyms you can think of.) If you still come up empty, ask your spouse, Christian friends, your pastor, a Sunday School teacher, or anyone else with whom you have a close relationship. God's promises apply to all kinds of situations, and He surely doesn't want you to go through life thinking there is no hope for one or more problems in your life.

Close this session with a personal prayer, sharing all your concerns with God. The first step in hope is making sure your relationship is right with Him. If you don't sense any peace immediately, don't give up. Keep praying regularly until you feel God's love penetrating your despair. God will work in your life. Just don't give up hope.

Bright Hope for Tomorrow

**KEY VERSE**

"*Those who hope in the Lord will renew their strength. They will soar on wings like eagles; they will run and not grow weary, they will walk and not be faint*" (Isaiah 40:31).

How does the loneliness section of the music store compare with the section of love songs?

3

IT'S LONELY AT THE BOTTOM

(Jeremiah 1—28)

Find a stopwatch or some other timepiece that can record seconds. You're going to need to time yourself for this activity. When you're ready, think of all the songs you can recall that dwell on love and togetherness. Spend 90 seconds and then quit. List your song titles below.

Now spend 90 seconds listing all the songs you can think of that deal with loneliness and solitude.

When you're finished, compare your lists and see which is longer. More than likely, your first list will be considerably longer than your second one. Sure, there have been some classic songs recorded about loneliness. ("Are You

37

Lonesome Tonight?" by Elvis and "Eleanor Rigby" by the Beatles are a couple of them.) But when it comes down to it, love and togetherness are more popular topics for songs, stories, etc., than loneliness and rejection. Yet it only figures that in millions of cases where loving relationships are broken (or where they never fully develop), the result is going to be loneliness.

Sometimes it's easy to get the impression that committed, godly people should never feel lonely. But that's not necessarily true. Even mature Christians can go through periods of solitude, depression, and loneliness. In this session, you'll see that while the main character didn't complain too much, he must have been a very lonely person at times.

JOURNEY ONWARD

This session and the next one will examine the life of Jeremiah, another of the prophets. The Book of Jeremiah is the longest in the Bible. (It has the most words—not the most chapters.) This book may seem a little confusing in places because it's not entirely in chronological order. But it's a fascinating book because it reveals so many of the personal struggles of its author.

Jeremiah must have been something of an expert on anguish and loneliness, because he is often referred to as "the weeping prophet." He brought basically the same message to Judah that Isaiah had proclaimed. But while Isaiah had lived about 100 years prior to the captivity he was prophesying, Jeremiah lived to see the exile come to pass. So Jeremiah's prophecies were urgent, specific warnings. Consequently, the kings and the people didn't want to hear them. And you'll see in this (and the next) session how Jeremiah's unpopularity caused him some persecution and suffering.

Read Jeremiah 1:1-10.
What was Jeremiah's occupation? (Jeremiah 1:1)

Who was king when Jeremiah became a prophet? (1:2)

It's Lonely at the Bottom

What do you remember about this king? (Review 2 Kings 22:1-2.)

This king also discovered the forgotten Book of the Law in the temple and renewed the covenant of obedience between God and the people of Judah. Jeremiah got along well with this good king, but his relationship with later kings was quite a different story.

How did Jeremiah become a prophet? (Jeremiah 1:4-10)

Visual Aids
Read Jeremiah 1:11-19.
God used a lot of object lessons with Jeremiah throughout his ministry to help teach him what would take place in the future. For example, one of the first visions God gave to Jeremiah was a branch of an almond tree (1:11-12). The almond tree was the first to bloom in the spring, so when the people saw the almond blooms they expected certain changes to occur. And God was definitely going to change their lifestyles. What was the second object lesson and explanation that God gave Jeremiah? (1:13-16)

What kept Jeremiah from being overly frightened by these visions? (1:17-19)

Skim Jeremiah 2:1–12:17.
God told Jeremiah many of the same things He had told Isaiah about the people of Judah. The people, who had at one time served God faithfully, had eventually forsaken God to worship many false gods. The illustration God used was that the Israelites were like a woman who had divorced her husband (3:1-25). Even after the tribes of Israel had already been taken into captivity, Judah continued to ignore the true God. So God was going to allow Judah to be captured as well. How widespread was the problem of sin in Judah? (5:1)

What kind of spiritual leadership were the people receiving? (6:13; 14:14)

Getting Personal — *What kind of spiritual leadership are you receiving?*

Since the spiritual condition of the people had deteriorated so much, what instructions did God give Jeremiah? (7:16-20)

Review Jeremiah 9:7. In effect, the people were leaving God no choice but to discipline them. Beyond a doubt, God loved His people. And because He loved them, He couldn't allow them to continue in such blatant disregard of what was best for them. So God was reluctantly going to allow them to suffer for a while so they would turn back to Him.

Jeremiah's message wasn't very well-received by the people of Judah. They just didn't want to hear what he had to say. But God was looking after His prophet. What was one of the things God did for Jeremiah? (11:18-23)

[NOTE: Anathoth was Jeremiah's hometown.]

As you might expect, Jeremiah went through some periods of doubt and depression. Like Job, Jeremiah wondered why God allowed the wicked to prosper. God assured Jeremiah that the wicked people would indeed be "uprooted" (12:14) and then would be returned if they had learned to put their trust in God (12:15-17). And God challenged Jeremiah to persevere. Review Jeremiah 12:5 and explain below what you think God's answer to Jeremiah meant.

It's Lonely at the Bottom

Read Jeremiah 13:1-27.
Later God used another object lesson with Jeremiah. What did God instruct Jeremiah to do? (13:1-5)

What happened? (13:6-7)

What message did the object lesson demonstrate? (13:8-11)

Then God gave another image. The people were very much aware that a wineskin was pretty useless unless it was filled with wine. But God could see that His nation was empty of all spiritual character. So He told Jeremiah that He was going to fill His "empty" nation with drunkenness, which would have a destructive effect on the wicked kings, priests, and prophets (13:12-14).

The people of Judah had become so sinful that they were practically beyond the point where they could change on their own. To what did God compare them? (13:23)

But God was going to deal with them in a severe way. What illustration did God use to describe how He would expose their sin? (13:26-27)

Getting Personal – *Has God ever exposed your sin? If so, how?*

Skim Jeremiah 14:1–20:18.
What did Jeremiah say was more deceitful than anything else? (17:9)

Then Jeremiah received yet another object lesson. Where did he go and what did he see? (18:1-4)

What was Jeremiah supposed to learn (and teach the people) from what he had seen? (18:5-6)

How were Jeremiah's messages being received at this time? (18:18)

God gave Jeremiah another object lesson to take before the people of Judah. What was Jeremiah supposed to do, and why? (19:1-3, 7-11)

How did the people respond to Jeremiah's object lesson? (20:1-2)

But Jeremiah just used his persecution as an opportunity to repeat God's message of forthcoming judgment on the people of Judah—and to personalize it for the person primarily responsible for giving him so much grief (20:3-6). You might think that since Jeremiah was beginning to get so much flak from the people, it would be better for him to keep quiet and lie low for a while. To be truthful, Jeremiah considered that option. So why didn't he choose to keep silent about God? (20:7-12)

King Zedekiah
Skim Jeremiah 21:1–25:38.
At this time, the ruler of Judah was King Zedekiah. When Babylonian King Nebuchadnezzar attacked Judah, Zedekiah wanted to know what Jeremiah

It's Lonely at the Bottom

thought would be the outcome. Zedekiah would have been a good example for the Session 2 discussion of someone with no concern for God, who just "hopes for the best." His attitude was, "Well, I know God has helped Judah out of some tight spots before. Maybe by some whim He will do it again" (21:2). The king had no faith—just blind hope. What was Jeremiah's response to Zedekiah? (21:3-7)

But God's message through Jeremiah didn't stop with Zedekiah. He also singled out kings Jehoahaz (Shallum), Jehoiakim, and Jehoiachin (Coniah) as examples of leaders who had no concern for God or God's people (Jeremiah 22). But Jeremiah went on to describe a coming King (Jesus). What kind of King would He be? (23:5-6)

God also told Jeremiah that the people were eventually going to have a new standard of God's faithfulness. Previously, people remembered God's power as they thought of how He had delivered them from Egypt. But what would future generations remember when they thought of God's faithfulness? (23:7-8)

One of the reasons Jeremiah was so unpopular was that God had told him that the people of Judah who cooperated with the Babylonians would be properly cared for and protected by God. But those who resisted (either by fighting it out in Jerusalem or running away to Egypt) would be unsuccessful in their attempts to escape Babylonian control. (Babylon was being used by God to bring Judah back to a proper relationship with Him. People who tried to avoid Babylonian rule were actually trying to dodge God's judgment on them.) What object lesson did God use to illustrate this to Jeremiah? (24:1-10)

How long would the captivity of Judah in Babylon last? (25:11)

What was going to eventually happen to Babylon? (25:12-14)

Flashback
Skim Jeremiah 26:1–27:17.
Jeremiah 26 tells of another of Jeremiah's close calls because the people didn't like his message. Even though it is recorded midway through his book, this event happened fairly early in his work as a prophet. (Remember that this book isn't entirely in chronological order.) What happened to Jeremiah? (26:1-3, 7-9)

Jeremiah avoided death when some of the older city officials recalled another prophet who had prophesied some of the same things Jeremiah had been saying. Which prophet was it? (26:17-18)

The city elders remembered that King Hezekiah had treated this other prophet with respect. They also recommended that Jeremiah not be harmed, so he was released. A prophet named Uriah, however, had not been so fortunate. He too had prophesied in the name of the Lord and had said many of the same things that Jeremiah said. When King Jehoiakim planned to put him to death, Uriah ran and hid in Egypt. But Jehoiakim's men followed him, brought him back, and killed him. So it's plain to see that it wasn't always easy to be a true prophet during this spiritually barren period of Judah's history.

At this point the Book of Jeremiah again jumps forward in time from the reign of Jehoiakim to the reign of Zedekiah (which puts Judah much closer to their captivity). And God again gave Jeremiah an object lesson for the people. What was Jeremiah supposed to do, and what was he supposed to tell the people of Judah? (27:1-6)

It's Lonely at the Bottom

But Jeremiah's message was disputed by a false prophet. A man named Hananiah publicly confronted Jeremiah in the temple. Jeremiah had told the people that the Babylonian captivity would be 70 years; how long did Hananiah say it would last? And what did Hananiah do to illustrate his message? (28:10-11)

What happened to Hananiah because he was deceiving the people of Judah? (28:12-17)

JOURNEY INWARD

As you can see, Jeremiah probably knew a lot about **loneliness**. Maybe you do too. So spend a few minutes now to see what you can learn about being lonely from a guy who was an expert. Below are a few observations, and you can add others of your own.

- *It doesn't help to whine.* Sure, Jeremiah often found himself alone in his work for God. But only in a couple of places do you see him complain. And those complaints weren't about his loneliness, but about his inability to understand why God was allowing certain things to happen.

- *Continual activity takes the focus off of loneliness.* Jeremiah always seemed to be doing something. You can't imagine him moping, sleeping late, or dwelling on the fact that he wasn't voted Most Popular. He knew what God wanted him to do, and he stayed busy.

- *He didn't compromise his principles to gain acceptance by others.* Jeremiah chose to proclaim his message boldly, even though he knew that to do so wouldn't make him any friends. Even when his life was at stake, he stuck to the absolute truth.

- *Though human friends were scarce, Jeremiah was satisfied to have a healthy relationship with God.* Perhaps this is the crucial key to combating loneliness. Jeremiah wasn't completely friendless. He was supported by some of the other prophets and elders, and by a close friend named Baruch (whom you will meet in the next session). Yet Jeremiah's major source of companionship seems to be God Himself. God has promised never to leave nor forsake His people (Joshua 1:5). So we should be confident that when we start to get lonely, He will be there to communicate with us. Even though there may be times when we have to stand alone (perhaps against a large crowd), God doesn't want us to feel lonely. He's right there with us.

What other observations did you make in this session about how Jeremiah dealt with loneliness? And how can you apply those observations to your own life?

To close this session, devise your own personal strategy to avoid loneliness. Use all the things you have noted so far, and write down a series of steps to take or things to do the next time you suffer from loneliness. Be as specific as you can. When you finish, ask God to help you recall your Strategy for Loneliness the next time you need it. And be assured that He will be there to comfort you, even if nobody else is around.

MY PERSONAL STRATEGY TO AVOID LONELINESS

It's Lonely at the Bottom

KEY VERSES

"Blessed is the man who trusts in the Lord, whose confidence is in Him. He will be like a tree planted by the water that sends out its roots by the stream. It does not fear when heat comes; its leaves are always green. It has no worries in a year of drought and never fails to bear fruit" (Jeremiah 17:7-8).

ROCKY GIBRALTAR

GINA THE HYENA

CRYING CHRISTINA

TIMID TIMOTHY

How do you think each of these people would respond to an emergency?

4

THE NEGATIVE EFFECTS OF TELL-A-VISION

(Jeremiah 29—52; Book of Lamentations)

It's interesting to watch the way different people react to emergencies. You may think someone is the most self-assured and confident person you've ever seen, but then he or she makes one little mistake and falls completely apart. Think of the people you know and see if any of them fit one of the following categories.

Rocky Gibraltar—Rocky's the kind of person that nothing seems to faze. Like the time when he broke his wrist playing racquetball, but finished the game and most of his nightly chores before he even said anything about the excruciating pain shooting through his upper arm. And Rocky's just as tough when it comes to showing emotions. He never cries, but then he doesn't laugh a lot either. In fact, it's usually hard to tell exactly what he's feeling, so he's not a lot of fun to be around.

Gina the Hyena—Gina is an extremely nervous person, who lets a lot of stuff get to her. So she has conditioned herself to laugh instead of cry, squeal, scream, or show any "negative" response to a crisis. When her supervisor gets on her case, she giggles. When her fiancé dumped her (and who could blame him?) she defiantly laughed in his face. Even when she passed a bad wreck on the highway, her nervous laugh popped out before she could say, "I hope no one is hurt." Gina just laughs her way through anything that goes wrong in her life—even though her laughter is only a cover for other emotions.

Crying Christina—Christina is just the opposite of Gina. Chris cries over every little thing that is out of the ordinary. She sobs when the Chicago Bulls

49

lose a basketball game. She weeps through most movies—even comedies. And when her parakeet died, stock in Kleenex rose three points.

Timid Timothy—Tim is as close to an ostrich as anyone you've ever seen. Whenever any crisis comes along, Timothy doesn't laugh, cry, or struggle with it. He runs for the nearest cover—his home, office, car, or wherever. He just can't seem to face bad things. You usually see him with a Walkman around his neck so he can tune out his surroundings at a minute's notice.

And then there's you. Give yourself a nickname to indicate the way you handle crises, and explain why you gave yourself that name.

JOURNEY ONWARD

If Jeremiah had had a nickname, it might have been Unjostled Jeremiah. It wouldn't have been Merry Jerry, because he didn't laugh his way through his rough spots. And neither should it be Jeremi-er the Crier (even though he is known as "the weeping prophet"). It's true that Jeremiah mourned the fate of Judah, but he never let his personal grief stand in the way of his presentation of God's message to the nation. No matter what happened to Jeremiah personally, or Judah as a whole, Jeremiah remained unjostled. He just continued to do his job. And it's that mixture of pain and perseverance that makes him such a remarkable person.

Read Jeremiah 29:1-32.
You should remember a number of close calls in the life of Jeremiah from the last session, but they aren't much to complain about in light of what the prophet is going to face in this session. Remember, we won't necessarily be going in chronological order through this session. In fact, we're going to start with a letter Jeremiah sent the people of Judah after they had been taken

The Negative Effects of Tell-a-Vision

into exile. What did God want His people to do during their captivity in Babylon? (Jeremiah 29:4-7)

What promise did God give them in Babylon? (29:10-14)

And as soon as Jeremiah established what God's plans were for the people of Judah in Babylon, God gave him a message for a false prophet. You may recall what happened to Hananiah in the last session (28:15-17). Well, another false prophet named Shemaiah was the same kind of person. He had been prophesying lies and condemning true prophets like Jeremiah. What did God say would happen to Shemaiah? (29:30-32)

Skim Jeremiah 30:1–35:19.
And to insure that people remembered who was telling the truth about the people's stay in Babylon, God gave Jeremiah a project. What was Jeremiah supposed to do? (30:1-3)

Jeremiah 30–31 contains a number of optimistic, motivating promises of God that He would definitely bring His people out of Captivity and renew His close relationship with them. Review these two chapters and note all the good things God promised to bring about. Especially notice the promise in 31:31-34. What special promise did God make?

Getting Personal – *What kinds of promises do you think God has made to you?*

Watchmen Who Wouldn't Quit

The Book of Jeremiah then goes back in time a bit, to the point right before the people of Judah were captured by the Babylonians. In fact, the Babylonians were just outside the city, about to take it over. Jeremiah was in custody of the state because he had prophesied that Judah would be defeated. He was confined and guarded, yet he had limited freedom to circulate and conduct business. And at this precise time, God gave Jeremiah an unusual command. What was Jeremiah supposed to do, and why might it seem like a strange request? (32:6-12)

By the way, this passage introduces Baruch, who was Jeremiah's aide (and probably his closest friend). What did Jeremiah tell Baruch was God's reasoning for asking him to do what he had just done? (32:13-15; see also vv. 42-44)

Then God gave Jeremiah a personal promise. What was it? (33:1-3)

For example, Jeremiah was well aware of the promises of God to return His people from Captivity. But God was farther ahead than that. What did God remind Jeremiah of? (33:14-18)

What message did God have for King Zedekiah? (34:1-5)

And then, right on the brink of God's judgment at the hands of the Babylonians, what did the people do to directly disobey God? (34:8-17)

The Negative Effects of Tell-a-Vision

Getting Personal — *When was the last time you directly disobeyed God? What were the circumstances?*

In contrast to the disobedient people of Judah were a tribe of nomads called the Recabites. What did God tell Jeremiah to invite the Recabites to do? (35:2)

Why didn't the Recabites accept Jeremiah's invitation? (35:5-11)

What did God want the people of Judah to learn from the Recabites? (35:12-16)

Flashback
Read Jeremiah 36:1-32.
Again, there is a flashback in the Book of Jeremiah. We go back to the reign of King Jehoiakim, when God gave Jeremiah an assignment. What was he to do? (36:1-3)

How did Jeremiah accomplish his assignment? (36:4-8)

When the people heard God's message, many of them believed it. (Remember that this was earlier in Jeremiah's ministry, before he had faced so much persecution.) The people knew the king might not be pleased by the message. So before they passed it on to Jehoiakim, they told Baruch and Jeremiah to hide. Then they took Jeremiah's scroll to the king. How did Jehoiakim respond to the reading of the scroll? (36:21-26)

What did Jeremiah do in response to the king's actions? (36:32)

Read Jeremiah 37:1-21.
Now the narrative returns to where it left off—the reign of King Zedekiah immediately before the Captivity. Jeremiah had predicted that the king wouldn't get the support he was expecting from Egypt to help him fight against the Babylonians. Then Jeremiah left Jerusalem to take care of some business in his hometown. But what did the king's representatives accuse him of doing? (37:13)

What happened to Jeremiah as a result? (37:14-21)

Read Jeremiah 38:1-28.
Other officials in Zedekiah's kingdom didn't appreciate Jeremiah's words advising the people of Judah to cooperate with the Babylonians. What did they want to happen to Jeremiah, and why? (38:4)

When the king turned over Jeremiah into their hands, what did the officials do with the prophet instead? (38:5-6)

How did Jeremiah get out of that personal crisis? (38:7-13)

Read Jeremiah 39:1-18.
Finally, the time came that Jeremiah had been prophesying so much about. The Babylonians broke through the wall of Jerusalem, and several of Nebuchadnezzar's key people immediately called a meeting at one of the gates. When Zedekiah saw the Babylonians inside the walls, he and the soldiers used another exit to leave the city in an attempt to escape. But they

didn't make it. What happened to Zedekiah? (39:4-8)

Nebuchadnezzar had heard of Jeremiah and had given instructions concerning him. What were the Babylonian soldiers supposed to do with Jeremiah? (39:11-14)

Skim Jeremiah 40:1–42:22.
What options did the Babylonians give Jeremiah? (40:2-5)

Jeremiah opted to stay in Judah under the authority of a man named Gedaliah (40:6), appointed by Nebuchadnezzar to represent Babylon. (The Babylonians carried off most of the people of Judah, but they left behind some of the poorest people. Jeremiah also stayed.) Before long, a plot was discovered against Gedaliah. Unfortunately, Gedaliah didn't believe the people who had discovered the plot, and he ignored their warnings (40:16). Sure enough, he and a number of his supporters were killed by a man named Ishmael (who had been one of King Zedekiah's officers).

The next day Ishmael killed some more people who showed up to meet with Gedaliah. He also took a number of people captive and headed for Ammonite country (41:10). Another man named Johanan discovered all the terrible things Ishmael had done and followed him. When he caught up with him, all the people taken forcibly by Ishmael gladly rallied around Johanan. But Ishmael got away (41:15).

Down to Egypt
Skim Jeremiah 42:1–43:13.
Johanan then decided to take his crew of people to Egypt to escape the Babylonians. On the way, they decided to ask Jeremiah what God wanted them to do, and they promised to do anything God said (42:5-6). What were God's instructions to the people? (42:7-16)

Watchmen Who Wouldn't Quit

How did the people respond to God's message? (43:1-7)

Notice that the people, acting in disobedience to God, carried Jeremiah and Baruch along with them. And even in Egypt, God gave Jeremiah an object lesson to pass along to the people. What did Jeremiah do, and what message did it symbolize? (43:8-13)

Read Jeremiah 44:1-30.
Not only had the people disobeyed God by going to Egypt instead of serving Babylon, they further rebelled against Him by making offerings to the gods of Egypt. What did Jeremiah say would happen to the people of Judah hiding out in Egypt? (44:11-14)

How did the people respond to Jeremiah? (44:15-17)

What did Jeremiah say would happen to Egypt? (44:30)

Skim Jeremiah 45:1–52:34.
The rest of the Book of Jeremiah contains a note of encouragement to Baruch (45:1-5), and a series of messages concerning different countries: Egypt (46:1-28), the Philistines (47:1-7), Moab (48:1-47), and a number of others (49:1-39). The final message is to Babylon (50–51). The basic theme is that even though God used Babylon to overpower Judah, Babylon would eventually be overtaken and Judah released. Who was to overpower Babylon? (51:11)

What was Jeremiah's final object lesson, which he used to demonstrate God's coming judgment on Babylon? (51:60-64)

Skim Lamentations 1:1–5:22.
The takeover of Jerusalem by Babylon is summarized in Jeremiah 52. (The account is very similar to 2 Kings 25.) But perhaps more important is the

The Negative Effects of Tell-a-Vision

effect the fall of Jerusalem had on the people of Judah, which is graphically portrayed in the Book of Lamentations. Jeremiah is believed to be the author of Lamentations, though the writer is not named. Reread the first two or three verses of Lamentations and describe what kind of mood the author was in.

The Babylonian takeover of Jerusalem wasn't pretty. In addition to the things you might expect (death, depression, etc.), what were some of the other horrendous things that happened? (Lamentations 2:20; 5:11-13)

But in spite of all the tragic events taking place in Judah and Jerusalem, the author of Lamentations hadn't given up on God. He knew that even though God had allowed many bad things to occur, He was still in control. The situation could have been much worse if God hadn't really cared about His people. What comfort did the author receive from God? (3:22-27)

Getting Personal — *What kind of comfort have you received from God?*

What assurance did the author have because of his knowledge of God's nature? (3:31-33)

What challenge did the author give? (3:39-42)

So you can see that even in the midst of an intense and painful crisis, trust in a loving God can bring great comfort. Even while Jeremiah's world was falling apart around him (literally!), he knew enough about God to realize that God was allowing this so His people would again learn to appreciate His love and protection. And some of the Bible's most precious promises about God come from the "judgmental" books of Jeremiah and Lamentations.

JOURNEY INWARD

How convinced are you that God really cares about you—even when He allows you to face long periods of hurting and sorrow? Sometimes we tend to give up on God during those times (when we really need Him the most). That's why it is important to learn from Jeremiah **how to handle a crisis.**

First, think of all the things in your own life that could be classified as a "crisis." List them below in the first column.

CRISIS	YOURS ALONE?	HOW MIGHT IT BE WORSE?

Now go back and put a check mark (√) in the second column if you are the only person you know of with that problem. And in the third column, think of ways that each crisis could be even worse.

As you evaluate the crises in your life, note that you probably aren't the only person in the world with those problems. And when you think about it, no matter how bad your crises might be at the moment, things probably *could* be worse.

Keep in mind that crises are a natural part of life. Jeremiah didn't seem particularly surprised that his life was less pleasant than he might want it to be. He didn't *enjoy* sinking into the slime at the bottom of the cistern, but at least he made it through the crisis with his life while other prophets had been killed. He surely didn't *like* the fact that he was a social outcast, but he knew his devotion to God was more important (in the long run) than his popularity with others.

The Negative Effects of Tell-a-Vision

What Jeremiah knew was that God would be there to see him through every crisis. He was smarter than to think he could be obedient to God *and* get along with everyone else (thereby avoiding many potential crises in his life). But sometimes *we* miss that point. Every life contains a number of crises, so the big question isn't whether or not you can dodge all the problems that come along. You can't. People you love will be injured or die. Some of your deepest hopes and dreams will never be accomplished. People you really like won't like you back.

So the more important question is whether or not you are letting God help you through your crises. Jeremiah suffered temporarily because he stood against the crowd and represented God. But when his prophecies came true and the Babylonians hit town, the "crowd" suffered while Jeremiah knew just where he stood. When you allow God to see you through crises, you benefit in the long run, no matter what you have to suffer on a short-term basis.

Of course, some crises *do* need immediate attention. As statistics show increasing numbers of young adults becoming victims of alcoholism, drug addiction, sexual abuse, and so forth, it is essential that those victims confront the problem head-on and do something about it as soon as possible. Yes, God will see us through any problems we have. But victims of such severe problems will probably also need counseling or some other kind of professional help. If you or someone you know is facing a serious crisis without knowing what to do about it, please notify a concerned pastor or a friend you trust. The healing process needs to begin right away, and you can be sure God will be with the person throughout the entire ordeal—and afterward.

Close this session with prayer, just to draw near to God and share your burdens with Him. You don't need to face your crises alone.

KEY VERSE
"Call to Me and I will answer you and tell you great and unsearchable things you do not know" (Jeremiah 33:3).

Most people have a fascination with the supernatural.

5
OUT OF THIS WORLD
(Ezekiel 1—18)

On the list that follows, check the appropriate box to indicate how often you participate in (or have participated in) each of the activities.

	NEVER	ONLY ONCE	SELDOM	REGULARLY
Palm Reading	❏	❏	❏	❏
Seances	❏	❏	❏	❏
Tarot Cards	❏	❏	❏	❏
Ouija Boards	❏	❏	❏	❏
Horoscopes	❏	❏	❏	❏
Astrological Readings	❏	❏	❏	❏
Fortune-telling	❏	❏	❏	❏
Ghost Stories	❏	❏	❏	❏
Eastern Meditation/ Chanting	❏	❏	❏	❏
Crystals/Channeling	❏	❏	❏	❏
Religions Other than Christianity	❏	❏	❏	❏
Fantasy Role-playing Games	❏	❏	❏	❏

Most people have some kind of fascination with the supernatural. Cheap supermarket tabloids regularly feature "news" articles about UFO sightings and alien encounters. Cultic religions occasionally gather their people together on hilltops to wait for the end of the world on a specific date (but they're all still waiting).

Someone has said that people are created with a God-shaped hole inside them. If they develop a personal relationship with God, they can find satisfaction with life. But those who refuse to believe in a personal, loving God will continue to attempt to fill that hole from other sources (like those mentioned above). And they will never be completely satisfied.

Now just because you may have participated in one or more of the previous activities doesn't mean you've deserted God. But regular involvement with any of these things can lead to a serious (and possibly dangerous) preoccupation with the supernatural. God has forbidden involvement with such activities (Deuteronomy 18:9-13). When people seek guidance or knowledge of the future from these sources, their involvement suggests that they are either dissatisfied or impatient with God's plans for their lives.

God isn't the only supernatural force in our universe. But He *is* the most powerful. He's also the one who loves you most, so it only makes sense to put your trust in Him and devote your energies to seeking His will for your life and your future.

JOURNEY ONWARD

This session takes us into the Book of Ezekiel, a prophet who was graphically aware of the supernatural forces around him (as you will soon see). Ezekiel was also painfully aware of what could happen when a group of people sought fulfillment in sources other than the true God.

You probably remember that Jeremiah did his prophesying just before and during the capture of Jerusalem by the Babylonians. He stayed in Judah while others of his people were carried off as captives to Babylon. Ezekiel was one of those people who was carried off. It was there in Babylon that God called him to be a prophet.

Ezekiel is easier to follow than some of the prophetic books because most of it is in chronological order. And the book is full of vivid visions and bold actions. Keep in mind that even though Nebuchadnezzar had entered Jerusalem and carried off captives, he had left behind people whom he had appointed to oversee the city. Jerusalem was still standing when Ezekiel and the others left. But seven years later, the city was destroyed (after Nebuchadnezzar's appointees rebelled and tried to form an alliance with Egypt). Ezekiel's message for the first half of his book (1–24) was that Jerusalem would fall. But after it did, Ezekiel wanted to assure the people that God would eventually lead them out of Captivity and back to their homeland (25–48).

Read Ezekiel 1:1-28.
What was Ezekiel's occupation? (Ezekiel 1:2-3)

Ezekiel hadn't been in exile long before God called him to be a prophet. And there was no doubt in Ezekiel's mind that he had been called. Review Ezekiel 1:4-21 and summarize the supernatural scene that Ezekiel witnessed.

Ezekiel recognized these creatures to be angels (10:20). And then he saw something else remarkable. What was it? (1:25-28)

Skim Ezekiel 2:1–7:27.
What was the first thing God told Ezekiel to do? (2:8–3:3)

God explained to Ezekiel that he was being sent to the stubborn, rebellious Israelites. Ezekiel was to faithfully relate God's messages to the people, whether they listened or not (2:5; 3:16-21). What did God tell Ezekiel so the prophet would be prepared for rejection? (3:7-9)

Getting Personal – *How prepared are you for rejection?*

How did Ezekiel respond to his first vision? (3:12-15)

God then gave Ezekiel a number of projects to do that would help him understand the judgment that was to come. What was Ezekiel's first project? (4:1-8)

Note that this project would not only make Ezekiel aware of the coming siege on Jerusalem; it also made him notice the degree of his nation's sin. And since this project would take about a year and two months, God wanted Ezekiel to prepare a quantity of water and food to ration during that time. At first, God told Ezekiel to prepare the food in the presence of the people, using human excrement as fuel (4:12). Why this strange request? (4:13)

But Ezekiel, being a priest who was very sensitive to whether something was "clean" or "unclean," balked at the idea of eating defiled food. So God allowed him to use cow manure as fuel instead (which still sounds gross to us, but it was used regularly as fuel during Ezekiel's time). What was the next symbolic project Ezekiel was instructed to conduct? (5:1-4)

What was the significance of Ezekiel's actions? (5:5, 12-13)

A View of Jerusalem
Skim Ezekiel 8:1–10:22.
Since God was instructing Ezekiel to prophesy against Jerusalem, He decided to show Ezekiel firsthand exactly how bad the conditions were in the city. But since Ezekiel was in Babylon, how did God show him the situation in Jerusalem? (8:1-4)

What improper forms of worship did Ezekiel see there? (8:5-16)

Getting Personal – *What improper forms of worship have you seen today?*

[NOTE: *Tammuz* was a Babylonian fertility god.]

God was going to pass judgment on the sinful people in Jerusalem. But He didn't just go in and wipe out the entire city. What did Ezekiel notice about how the righteous people were protected from God's wrath? (9:1-6, 11)

Because of God's judgment on the people, what happened to the temple? (9:7)

What other significant event took place in regard to the temple? (10:1-5, 18-19)

Read Ezekiel 11:1-25.
As a priest, Ezekiel would have been especially sensitive to seeing the glory of God leaving the temple. God's presence in the temple was an assurance to the people of Israel that He was with them. But now He was symbolically showing the removal of His blessing from the people who refused to honor Him. The following chapter shows some more of the reasons the people were ignoring God. What boast were the evil leaders making? (11:1-4)

Their boast sounds a little strange. But the meaning of their comparison is that they were the major "ingredients" of Jerusalem (which was symbolized by the pot). But God disagreed with their analysis. Who did God say was the real "meat" in the pot? (11:7, 11)

How did God emphasize what He was prophesying through Ezekiel? (11:13)

What promise did God repeat to Ezekiel? (11:16-17)

Back to Babylon
Read Ezekiel 12:1-28.
Then Ezekiel, in his vision, returned to the exiled people in Babylon where he told them what God had shown him. And before long, God gave Ezekiel another project to do. What was Ezekiel asked to do this time? (12:3-7)

What was the significance of Ezekiel's actions? (12:10-12)

The people of Judah had a popular saying just prior to their exile, and God told Ezekiel that He was going to put an end to it. What was the proverb? (12:21-23)

Read Ezekiel 13:1–15:8.
God told Ezekiel to prophesy against the false prophets in Judah. What lies had the false prophets been telling the people? (13:6, 10)

Besides the false prophets, at whom was God angry? (13:18-21)

God told Ezekiel that the situation in Judah was so bad that no one could intercede on their behalf this time. God even singled out three people noted for their faithfulness, saying that not even those three people (if they had still

Out of This World

been around) could convince Him to keep Judah from facing judgment. Who were the three righteous people God had in mind during this sinful period of Judah's history? (14:12-14, 19-20)

God often spoke of Israel and Judah as a vine. He had pointed out through Isaiah (5:1-7) and Jeremiah (2:20-21) that the nation was not bearing good fruit. But now, through Ezekiel, God said that Judah the vine was not good for anything. The purpose of a vine is to bear fruit. If people want good wood, they get it from a tree. So what is the eventual outcome of a vine that refuses to bear fruit? (Ezekiel 15:1-6)

Getting Personal — *Are you bearing fruit? Why or why not?*

Read Ezekiel 16:1-63.
Israel (and later Judah) was very proud of its capital city, Jerusalem. The city was old and had existed long before King David conquered it and made it the center of government and worship in Israel. With God's leadership, Jerusalem had become a showplace of grandeur, beauty, and wisdom. What illustration did God use to describe to the people of Israel how much He had cared for the city? (16:1-14)

How had the people responded to God's care? (16:15-22)

After God accused Jerusalem of prostitution, He pointed out that the people even lacked the wisdom of prostitutes. Why? (16:32-34)

So what was God (the husband) going to allow to happen to Jerusalem (the unfaithful wife)? (16:35-42)

Skim Ezekiel 17:1–18:32.
God then gave Ezekiel another illustration to pass on to the people of Israel. Summarize the parable God told to Ezekiel (17:1-10)

What was the meaning of the parable? (17:11-18)

God made a promise by adding to the parable He had just told. What was God's symbolic promise, and what do you think it meant? (17:22-24)

God wanted to straighten out another misconception held by the people of Judah. They were quoting another proverb (different from the one quoted in 12:21) that wasn't entirely correct. What was this second proverb? (18:1-2)

When Job was suffering, he had referred to a similar saying (Job 21:19). Jeremiah was familiar with it as well (Jeremiah 31:29). And there was a certain amount of truth to the thought that one generation's sins could have an effect on future generations. You may remember instances from your study of *Who's Running This Kingdom?* where God's judgment on one person was postponed and applied instead to later members of his household—but always in cases where they deserved such treatment. (Review 1 Kings 11:9-12 and 21:25-29 for specific examples.)

But in Ezekiel's time, the proverb was being used by people who represented the worst era of Israel's history. And the common use of this proverb made it easy for the people to think one of two things: (1) We can blame our ancestors for all these judgments that God is threatening us with, or (2) If we lead sinful lives, we shouldn't worry too much because God may decide to punish some of our descendants rather than us. What did God make clear to these people? (Ezekiel 18:3-4)

What did God want the people to do? (18:30-32)

In the next session, you will see God's judgment come to pass on the city of Jerusalem—the judgment that had been prophesied so often by Isaiah, Jeremiah, and Ezekiel. As predicted, it would prompt the repentance of the people. It's too bad they had to learn the hard way to listen to what God had to tell them. But then, there are plenty of times when we disobey God's instructions and learn too late that those instructions were for our own good. That's why we need to spend a few minutes thinking about the supernatural aspect of God.

JOURNEY INWARD

As you complete this session, spend a while thinking about the **supernatural** element of your faith. Sure, you know in your head that God is all-knowing, all-powerful, and present everywhere. But how do those facts affect your day-to-day life?

Remember that Ezekiel was a priest. His entire life centered on attending to the things of God. Yet it was not until he was taken away to Babylon that Ezekiel got a close look at who God really is. And surely that vision of God in His glory, surrounded by some of His angels, had an impact on the prophet's level of devotion to God.

If you don't think too often about what God is really like, it's easy to overlook His true nature. If we envision Him as "our friend in the sky," a doddering old grandfather, a gift-giver, or in other similar roles, we miss out on a lot. It's true that through Jesus we can be the friends of God (John 15:15) and receive His good gifts (James 1:17). But unless we occasionally dwell on His magnificent holiness and consider the multitude of ways that God is superior to any other force in the universe, we will never really feel secure in His power and forgiveness. So spend a few quiet minutes right now, letting your mind try to comprehend the glory of God. As you do, praise Him for who He is.

When you finish, take a few more minutes to consider what effect God's supernatural nature should be having on your life. For example, if you regularly began to think of God as the Person in Ezekiel's visions, how would your life be different? Or suppose God had shown Himself to *you* instead of Ezekiel. How might each of the following things change:

❑ Your prayer times and spiritual life?

❑ Your relationships with other people?

❑ Your fears?

❑ Your priorities?

❑ Your attitudes?

❑ Your thoughts?

❑ Other parts of your life?

Out of This World

Some people try to live their lives based on an ever-changing alignment of stars. Some seek advice from the spirit world. Others look to Buddha, Mohammed, or similar spiritual leaders who are now dead. Doesn't it make more sense to search for truth and wisdom by consulting the living God who created the stars and reigns supreme over the spirit world? When it comes to supernatural help, He should become your natural choice.

KEY VERSE

"This is what the Sovereign Lord says: Repent! Turn from your idols and renounce all your detestable practices" (Ezekiel 14:6).

What a lousy end to what was supposed to be a perfect day!

6
WHO'S RESPONSIBLE HERE?
(Ezekial 19—48)

You're on the treadmill. Depressed. Mad at the world. What a lousy end to what was supposed to be a perfect day. And it wasn't even your fault. Well, not really.

For months you had planned to spend today at the lake with some of your girlfriends. The canoes had been rented, travel arrangements were set, your husband was going to baby-sit, and all that was left to do was wake up this morning and go. Of course, you awoke early.

But when you went to wash your face, there was no water in the bathroom. As you checked it out, you saw your husband wading through your basement. Something had gone wrong with the water heater, and he had disconnected the water to find the problem. Your teenage daughter was also a little on the frantic side. She was having a party in the afternoon, and the water situation had "dampened" her plans. Suddenly, you were the only person around who didn't have anything important to do (so they thought).

Your husband handed you a small, weird-looking part and sent you to the hardware shop to look for a new one. As you shoved it into your pocket, your daughter gave you a quickly prepared shopping list of last-minute items she needed. Your son wanted a ride to Little League practice. And since you hadn't had benefit of a shower or shampoo, you looked like a Neanderthal. You would have protested these unscheduled errands, but you really needed to get to a bathroom that worked.

So off you went. You figured you could time things about right to get home a half-hour before you were supposed to leave for your trip. So first to the hardware store. Oops. Make that the gas station. Besides your need to borrow a bathroom, you had neglected to fill up last night. Add 10 minutes to your schedule. And then when you got to the hardware store, you discovered it wouldn't open for another 15 minutes. Forget that. Off to Little League and then the grocery store.

Now did your daughter want "toothpaste" or "toothpicks"? "Cheetos" or "Cheerios"? You would get some of each, but you're short of money from your stop at the gas station. There's no time to call and check, so you go with the toothpaste and Cheerios. As you race your cart up and down the aisles, you frighten more than one little old lady with your crazed look of desperation. And with the milk, soft drinks, and a few more bulky items, you see that you're going to have to make more than one trip to unload when you get home.

Your return visit to the hardware store is short and sweet. You pocket the new part along with the old one. But traffic is slowed down by a wreck on your way home, and you almost cause another one as you see that your ride is going to be at your house to pick you up any minute now.

You whip into your driveway, make the three trips into the kitchen with the groceries, see that your girlfriends are there, grab your stuff, and shout goodbye. You're none too happy with your family for making you go through all that on a day that was supposed to be all fun. You especially don't like the fact that you still look like a Neanderthal. (Guess you'll have to wear that silly-looking hat all day now.)

The minute you get to the lake, you reach into your pocket for your sunglasses and find instead a couple of water heater parts. You spend the rest of the day feeling bad (and guilty), and when you get home you get the silent treatment from your husband for "showing such a lack of responsibility." What you didn't expect was more grief from your daughter. ("Now why in the world do you think my friends would be interested in toothpaste and Cheerios?")

Sure, you tried to explain to your family that they had piled a lot of that responsibility on you suddenly and unexpectedly. But they just made you feel like you didn't care at all about them. (To be honest, right now you were having your doubts.) But you *do* care about your family. It's just that, well, was it fair for them to expect you to do everything they wanted instead of what you wanted to do?

JOURNEY ONWARD

One of life's harsh realities is that you don't always get to do everything you want to do. You share your world with about four billion people (give or take a couple of billion), and you have a certain responsibility to the other 3,999,999,999. When you get a new car, for instance, it might sound tempting to "take it out and see what this baby can do." But you need to remember that you share the roads with elderly drivers, women and children pedestrians, and other people test-driving *their* new cars. You are accountable to those people to drive safely.

You also have certain responsibilities to your family and to God. You can be sure that sometimes those responsibilities will clash with your own personal priorities. Usually, the more you try to avoid your responsibilities, the more you will suffer for it.

In this session you will discover a number of examples that pertain to responsibility and accountability. Some are positive examples and others are negative. As you go through the session, jot down anything that comes to mind from your life that pertains to these topics. You'll have the opportunity to evaluate them in the **Journey Inward** section.

Skim Ezekiel 19:1–24:27.

You should remember that the people of Judah had gotten to the point where they totally neglected their accountability to God. So Ezekiel was actively prophesying that Jerusalem would fall at the hands of the Babylonians. Ezekiel 19–20 summarizes the specific ways that Israel had acted irresponsibly toward God (expressed symbolically in chapter 19 and directly in chapter 20).

It's interesting to see that God knew exactly what was going to happen, but He was going to let the Babylonian king decide what to do through his usual customs of "random" selection and omens. Specifically, how would the king of Babylon decide to attack Jerusalem? (21:18-23)

[NOTE: Examination of sheep livers was one method the Babylonians (and later the Romans) used for telling the future.]

Repeating one of the illustrations from the last session, Ezekiel identified the cause of Israel's spiritual decline. Israel (Samaria) and Judah (Jerusalem) were symbolized by two sisters named Oholah and Oholibah. What sinful practice were these "sisters" guilty of? (23:1-4)

With whom did the two sisters participate in their sin? (23:5-21)

The irresponsibility of Israel and Judah had even reached the point where the people were sacrificing their own children to the idols of the other nations (23:36-39). So God was going to chastise Israel and Judah. What punishment was in store for them? (23:44-49)

Another image repeated from Session 5 is found in Ezekiel 24, where the city of Jerusalem is compared to a cooking pot. (Review Ezekiel 11, especially v. 3.) The people of Judah who left Jerusalem had been taken away by the Babylonians in 597 B.C. It seems that some of the people who didn't get taken away thought they were pretty hot stuff (the "meat" in the pot). But what did God say would happen to the ingredients of the pot? (24:6)

Who's Responsible Here?

What was to happen to the pot itself (the city of Jerusalem)? (24:9-13)

[The image of "purity by fire" turned out to be a good one. The Babylonians broke through the walls of Jerusalem in July, 586 B.C. And in August of that year, the city was literally burned. Keep in mind, however, that this event has not yet taken place in Ezekiel's narrative.]

God knew the temple would also be destroyed as Jerusalem fell. The temple had been His people's primary source of contact with Him, yet they were taking for granted His presence among them. So it was at this time that something happened to Ezekiel to parallel and illustrate the tragic separation of God's temple from the people. What happened to Ezekiel? (24:15-18)

Getting Personal – *Have you ever taken God's presence in your life for granted? What was the result?*

God had instructed Ezekiel not to mourn publicly. Why not? (24:19-24)

Turning Point
Skim Ezekiel 25:1–32:32.
At this point the message of Ezekiel begins to change. Ezekiel's personal tragedy and the fall of Jerusalem (a national tragedy) were turning points. God had previously forecast judgment on His people, and He had allowed it to come to pass. But as soon as it took place, God began to focus on forgiveness and restoration.

Watchmen Who Wouldn't Quit

God had allowed other aggressive nations to overpower the people of Israel and Judah. But He wasn't going to allow them to celebrate in their selfish conquests for very long. Like Isaiah and Jeremiah had done before him, Ezekiel made a number of prophecies against those nations—the Ammonites, Moabites, Edomites, Philistines, Egyptians, and others (Ezekiel 25–32).

One of the "others" was a city named Tyre, the capital of Phoenicia. Ezekiel first described the bad things that would happen to Tyre (26–27), and then addressed the "king" of Tyre (28:12). Some people believe that this part of the prophecy (like Isaiah's words in Isaiah 14:12-17) is a reference to Satan. Review Ezekiel 28:11-19 and jot down some of the things that might suggest that the passage refers to Satan.

Read Ezekiel 33:1-33.
Of course, whether or not Ezekiel's prophecy was also a reference to Satan, it definitely reflected the problem of pride displayed by the leader of Tyre (as well as leaders of surrounding ungodly nations).

Session 5 mentioned that Ezekiel had a position similar to that of a watchman (3:17). When can a watchman be held responsible for harm that comes to a city? (33:6-8)

When is a watchman not accountable for the harm that comes to his city? (33:9)

Who's Responsible Here?

How do you think these instructions applied to Ezekiel?

At this point in Ezekiel's book, the exiles in Babylon received official word of the fall of Jerusalem. God had previously given Ezekiel a way to tell when Jerusalem had been destroyed. What was the sign? (24:25-27; 33:21-22)

Even after Jerusalem was destroyed, there were still people in the area who refused to accept the action as God's judgment. They were foolishly optimistic enough to believe they should remain in control of the land (33:23-26). But God declared that the remaining people would be killed and the land made desolate (33:27-29). The problem with the people was that they never made themselves accountable to God or to Ezekiel, who had repeatedly warned them not to try to avoid the exile to Babylon. How had the people been responding to Ezekiel's messages? (33:31-32)

Skim Ezekiel 34:1–39:29.
What comparison did God use to describe the leaders of Judah who were misleading the people? (34:1-6)

How does God's leadership differ from the corrupt leadership in Judah? Be specific. (34:11-16)

What was God planning to do for His people, and why? (36:22-27)

What vision did God give Ezekiel to illustrate what He was going to do for His people? (37:1-14)

And God also revealed His long-range plans to Ezekiel (and the Israelites). What did God tell Ezekiel to do? (37:15-19)

Keep in mind that Israel and Judah had been separate nations since shortly after the death of Solomon (about 931 B.C.). It wasn't really God's intention that they split—they were all His people. But as the kings began to think more of themselves than they did God's plans, they perpetuated the division of the two kingdoms. What were God's future plans for His people? (37:20-23)

How is God going to avoid the same problem of kings who look more to their own interests than to God's? (37:24-25)

Who's Responsible Here?

Getting Personal — *Do you ever look more to your own interests than to God's? Why or why not?*

But just the fact that God was bringing His people back together again didn't mean they wouldn't face further opposition. Ezekiel prophesied an attack from the north led by a king named Gog from a land called Magog (38:1-16). What will be the result of that attack? (38:18–39:10)

Skim Ezekiel 40:1–48:35.
Ezekiel's final recorded vision was an extended one that is described in chapters 40–48. (It occurred 14 years after the fall of Jerusalem.) What was the first thing Ezekiel saw in this vision? (40:1-3)

The next chapters provide Ezekiel's description as he followed the man around and recorded the measurements of a temple. This may seem unusual, since the temple in Jerusalem had just been torn down. And there is some discussion as to what temple Ezekiel was observing, but most scholars seem to think that this temple is yet to be built. The dimensions don't fit Herod's temple (which eventually replaced Solomon's temple after its destruction), so perhaps Ezekiel's vision was of the temple to be used during a reign of Jesus yet to occur. A 1,000-year reign is mentioned in Revelation 20:1-6, a passage which happens to be followed by a mention of Gog and Magog (Revelation 20:7-8; Ezekiel 38–39).

As Ezekiel checked out the "man" who was doing the measuring, he noticed that the man had a rod (for shorter measurements) and a linen cord (for longer ones). If you want to compute the distances as you read through this section, you need to use a different measurement for a "cubit." Previously, one cubit was equal to 18 inches. But this section of Ezekiel records distances in "long cubits" (about 21 inches). So the rod in the man's hand which was "six long cubits" (40:5) was about 10 1/2 feet long.

Review Ezekiel 40–48. As you do, try to match the description of the parts of the temple with the floor plan shown here.

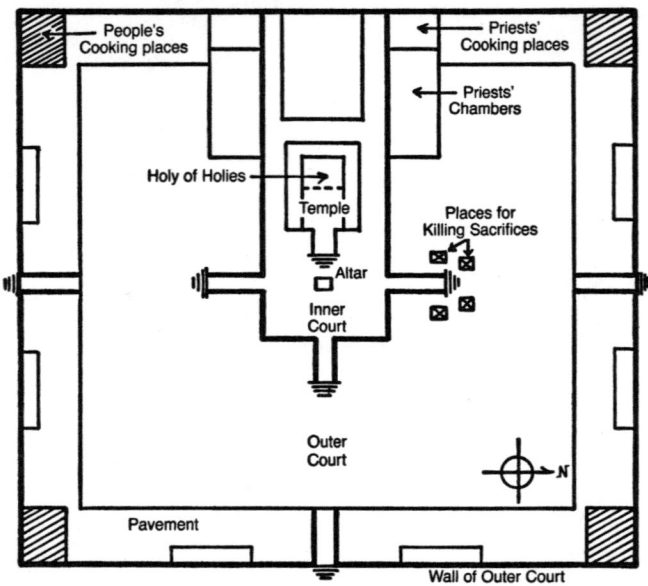

Ezekiel had previously witnessed something leave the old temple that he here saw return to the new one. What did he see? (43:1-5; review 10:4, 18)

The new temple was also the source of an unusual body of water. What did Ezekiel see coming from the temple? (47:1-5)

Who's Responsible Here?

What effect did this water have on other bodies of water? (47:6-10)

As you skim through this section, you should also note that God is still interested in the division of land among His people (45:1-12; 47:13–48:29). Way back in the Book of Genesis, God had promised this land to Abraham as "an everlasting possession to you and your descendants after you" (Genesis 17:8). And even though the Israelites had repeatedly let God down in the areas of responsibility and accountability, God's promises to His people are sure and certain. This fact comes through in the naming of the new city that Ezekiel witnessed. What will be the name of the city in which the new temple is located? (Ezekiel 48:35)

JOURNEY INWARD

As you went through this session, did you notice anything referring to **responsibility and accountability** that can also apply to your own life? The Book of Ezekiel speaks to several relevant areas: the people's accountability (as a nation) to God, Ezekiel's responsibility to pass along the messages given him by God, each individual's responsibility to listen to God's messengers, and so forth. These spiritual matters are indeed important, but they are by no means the only areas that require your accountability. You have obligations to your family, friends, community, and job (if you have one). And if you aren't showing responsibility in each of these areas, you aren't likely to develop accountability in church matters.

So on the following Performance Review, give yourself a grade that reflects your accountability in each area. Be honest. Sometimes when you're evaluating yourself, it's easy to either give yourself the benefit of the doubt or to be too hard on yourself. But be as fair as you can.

PERFORMANCE REVIEW

AREA OF PERFORMANCE   UNSATISFACTORY   SATISFACTORY

Family Life
- ❏ Gets along with spouse
- ❏ Gets along with children
- ❏ Completes chores

Friendship Development
- ❏ Loyal to friends
- ❏ Willing to make new friends
- ❏ Equal treatment of different friends
- ❏ Sets good examples for friends

Job Responsibilities
- ❏ Respect for boss and coworkers
- ❏ Honest when recording time worked
- ❏ Responsible with employer's supplies
- ❏ Works for employer as if for God (Colossians 3:23-24)
- ❏ Willing Attitude

Church Accountability
- ❏ Personal prayer life
- ❏ Personal Bible study
- ❏ Supports other church members
- ❏ Financially supports church activities
- ❏ Involved in church, Sunday School, and/or group meetings
- ❏ Maintains relationship with God

Hopefully, your Performance Review will point out the places where you are excelling in being a responsible person. It should also let you know where you could stand some improvement. As much as you might want to live your own life and have everyone else leave you alone, you aren't entitled to that right. We all have many responsibilities to a number of people. And we need to become more dependent on each other. The New Testament model is that of a human body, with a variety of parts that provide different talents and responsibilities. God hasn't chosen to give every Christian every gift he or she needs to get along in the world. We need each other, and we all need to be accountable to Jesus, who is the head of the body (see 1 Corinthians 12:12-31).

Spend some time this week reevaluating your accountability to the people around you and to God. Focus especially on the areas where you rated yourself low on your Performance Review. It may be hard at first to sacrifice your own desires in order to be more responsible to others, but it's a change that will have a long-lasting effect on your life. Try it and see.

KEY VERSE

"I will give you a new heart and put a new spirit in you; I will remove from you your heart of stone and give you a heart of flesh" (Ezekiel 36:26).

*Paul's friends really wanted to be accepted by their peers,
so they started acting a lot differently.*

7

WHEN THE HEAT IS ON
(Daniel 1—5)

Paul was confused. He and his group of friends had been so close in college that he didn't think anything could ever destroy their friendship. In fact, they had done all those goofy things that young fraternity brothers do. And it was just months ago that they were committed to remaining lifelong friends.

But soon after they all graduated and began their careers, things began to change. Most of Paul's friends really wanted to be accepted by their peers at work, so they started acting a lot differently. They first started going to parties where there was heavy drinking and smoking (and probably drugs, Paul suspected). Their conversation topics shifted from sports and business opportunities to sexual themes and how to look and dress "just right" to impress other people. They still accepted Paul as a friend, but the closeness between them was disappearing. And even though Paul hadn't yet begun to change his lifestyle, he was feeling more and more pressure to do so.

If you were an impartial third party observing this situation, what would you advise Paul to do?

Have you ever been in a similar situation? If so, briefly recall the facts and the way you felt. Use the space below.

It will help to keep your situation in mind as you go through this session. Peer pressure is nothing new. Lots of nice people have turned into hypocrites, stuck-up snobs, back-stabbing traitors, and other assorted monsters because of peer pressure. It's unusual to find people who show no signs at all of weakening. Yet in this session, you will discover a number of people whose trust in God prevented any bit of wavering because of peer pressure, even when their lives and careers are threatened because of their nonconformity.

JOURNEY ONWARD

This session should provide a breath of fresh air for a number of reasons. First, it's about Daniel—a prophet you've actually heard of and know something about. Second, we're not going to try to cover dozens of chapters in a single session. In the first six sessions of this book, you've probably worn yourself out just turning pages in your Bible. From here on, the amount of content becomes a little more reasonable. And third, you are going to get to review some classic Bible stories in light of the new things you've been learning about Judah's captivity in Babylon. You should come away from this session with a better understanding of exactly what kind of people Daniel and his friends were.

Read Daniel 1:1-21.
You already know that when the Babylonians conquered Jerusalem, they carried away a number of the people of Judah. But the Babylonians singled out some of the people for a special assignment. What were the specially selected people supposed to do? (Daniel 1:1-4)

What privileges did these people have? (1:5)

Of all the people who were selected, which ones were so special that their names were recorded here? Give both their real names and their new Babylonian names. (1:6-7)

When the Heat Is On

The name changes were significant. Originally, the names of all these people reflected a characteristic of God (Daniel = "God is my judge"; Hananiah = "The Lord shows grace"; Mishael = "Who is what God is?"; Azariah = "The Lord helps"). The new Babylonian names made statements too—not about Israel's God, but about a number of Babylonian gods.

But the fact that the Babylonians were calling Daniel and his friends by other names didn't make them different people. They were still loyal to the God of Israel and Judah. How do you know? (1:8)

Getting Personal — *How do people know that you are loyal to God?*

Even though the Babylonian guy in charge liked Daniel and wanted to comply with his request, there was a problem. What was the Babylonian officer worried about? (1:9-10)

At this point, Daniel had several choices. He could have told the Babylonian officer to forget about including him in the special program. He could have insisted on doing things his own way. He could have made a lot of trouble for the officer, since he knew the guy was afraid of his boss. But Daniel did none of these things. What did Daniel do instead? (1:11-14)

What was the result? (1:15-16)

Not only did Daniel and his friends prosper physically from their loyalty to God, they received special spiritual awareness as well. What was special about them? (1:17-20)

Daniel Dream-Teller
Read Daniel 2:1-49.
It wasn't long before Daniel had the opportunity to use his special gifts. There were a number of problems in the kingdom. What was King Nebuchadnezzar's problem? (2:1-3)

What problem did the king's servants have? (2:4-6)

These servants really wanted to help the king, but he was making it a little difficult for them. What unreasonable request did the king make? (2:7-11)

When the servants were unable to fulfill the king's expectations, what was Nebuchadnezzar going to do? (2:12-13)

But then came Daniel to the rescue. How did Daniel handle this touchy situation? (2:14-18—Notice both his actions and his attitudes.)

How was Daniel able to accomplish the king's seemingly impossible request? (2:19)

What was the first thing Daniel did after he discovered how to answer the Babylonian king? (2:19-23)

How did Daniel explain his ability to interpret dreams when he was before Nebuchadnezzar? (2:24-30)

When the Heat Is On

Describe Nebuchadnezzar's dream. (2:31-35)

Getting Personal — *Have you ever had a dream that seemed significant? What was important about it?*

The dream was simple enough, but the explanation was a little more complex. Daniel foretold a series of nations to come that would stand as world powers. Nebuchadnezzar and Babylon were represented by the head of gold. But Daniel could see an inferior nation overpowering Babylon and taking control. Beyond that, a third and a fourth major power would come to rule. Most people believe the succession of nations following Babylon to be the Medo-Persian Empire, followed by the Greek Empire, followed by the Roman Empire.

But Daniel saw beyond these world empires to a "rock" that would overpower and replace them all. What did the rock represent? (2:44-45)

What things did King Nebuchadnezzar do in response to Daniel's reconstruction and interpretation of his dream? (2:46-49)

Read Daniel 3:1-6.
Nebuchadnezzar was impressed with the God that Daniel served. The king admired God's ability to reveal such mysteries. But it was obvious from his next move that Nebuchadnezzar wasn't yet ready to acknowledge God as the only one worthy of praise. What did Nebuchadnezzar do? (3:1-6)

Fiery Furnace
Read Daniel 3:7-30.
Clearly, it would be hard for godly people to willingly follow the king's

command. Yet apparently many of the Jewish people who had been taken to Babylon were giving in under the pressure. (After all, the threat of being thrown alive into a blazing furnace [3:6] was good incentive not to disobey.) But Shadrach, Meshach, and Abednego refused to be pressured into doing something they knew wasn't right.

As soon as the three of them were seen disobeying the king's order, a bunch of tattletale astrologers went running to Nebuchadnezzar. How did the king respond when he discovered that some of his own administrators were ignoring a direct order? (3:8-13)

Even in the king's agitated state, he was willing to give Shadrach, Meshach, and Abednego a second opportunity to conform. But this time he made it very clear that disobedience would definitely result in a tour through the fiery furnace. And the response of the three young Hebrew men was very interesting. What did they tell the king? (3:16-18)

Their response was not what Nebuchadnezzar was ready to hear, and he really went off the deep end. What instructions did he give? (3:19-20)

What clue is given as to exactly how hot the fire was? (3:22)

Whatever Nebuchadnezzar expected to see next, he didn't see it. What *did* he observe after Shadrach, Meshach, and Abednego were thrown into the fiery furnace? (3:24-25)

What effect did this miracle have on King Nebuchadnezzar? (3:26-30)

When the Heat Is On

Read Daniel 4:1-37.
Nebuchadnezzar was reluctantly beginning to realize what kind of God he was dealing with. But he still needed another lesson—this time on a more personal level. Again God sent a dream to Nebuchadnezzar to alert him to future events, and again Daniel had to interpret for the king. What was Nebuchadnezzar's dream this time? (4:9-18)

What was Daniel's interpretation of the dream? (4:19-27)

Everything that Daniel predicted came true. It all started one day when King Nebuchadnezzar was strolling around on the roof of his palace and proudly claimed that *he* was responsible for making Babylon the great empire it was. What happened to him then? (4:28-33)

How did Nebuchadnezzar's experience affect his attitude toward God? (4:34-37)

Writing on the Wall
Read Daniel 5:1-31.
But even after Nebuchadnezzar learned to acknowledge God as the source of all good things, his successors still needed to learn the same lesson. One of Nebuchadnezzar's descendants who ruled Babylon was a man named Belshazzar. (Don't confuse this name with Daniel's Babylonian name, Belteshazzar.) King Belshazzar was throwing a big party one day. Thousands were in attendance. There was eating and drinking and all kinds of merrymaking—including a lot of worship of the Babylonian gods. But suddenly a highly unusual occurrence brought the party to a screeching halt. What put a damper on the festive atmosphere? (5:1-6)

It seems that Belshazzar's wise men weren't much wiser than Nebuchadnezzar's wise men had been. (Maybe they were the same dumb guys.) None of them had any idea how to solve the king's problem. How was the king responding to this crisis? (5:7-8)

But eventually one of the queens remembered Daniel, and told Belshazzar of his ability to "interpret dreams, explain riddles, and solve difficult problems" (5:12). So Daniel was summoned and asked to explain the writing. But before he did, he reminded Belshazzar of when Nebuchadnezzar had refused to humble himself before God and was made to live the life of a wild animal for several years. Why did Daniel bring this event up to Belshazzar? (5:22-24)

What was the meaning of the message that the hand had written on the wall? (5:25-28)

What happened to Daniel as a result of his interpretation of the writing on the wall? (5:29)

How long was it before the message on the wall came true? (5:30)

As Darius the Mede defeated Babylonian King Belshazzar, Daniel's interpretation of Nebuchadnezzar's dream about the statue began to come true. Babylon fell at the hands of the Medo-Persian Empire.

It's more than apparent that Daniel was pretty good at dealing with other people's problems and other people's dreams. In the next session, you will see how he handles his own problems and dreams.

JOURNEY INWARD

As you read through the opening chapters of Daniel, it's a natural place to focus on the topic of **peer pressure**. It may help to put yourself in Daniel's sandals. Imagine you are carried away from your own country as a prisoner. Then you discover that you are one of just a few people who is qualified to be trained for special service in your new country. This position will entitle you to a good education, training for an important job, and many other privileges. The only catch is that you have to do a couple of things that you're uncomfortable with.

Most of us in such a situation would probably let our personal convictions slip a little bit. We might even try to justify our decision and excuse our behavior by thinking that we could change things once we had gained some power. Or maybe we would be defiant from the first, and tell the other people that there is no way that we would ever go along with their offer. But Daniel took neither of these approaches. He cooperated with others as much as he could, and he stood firm when those people threatened to violate his personal principles. But notice *how* he stood firm. He didn't provoke the others or try to convince them all to come around to his way of thinking. Rather, he challenged them to let him try his way for a specific period of time to see if it didn't work better than what they were doing. And of course, God was with Daniel and made it apparent to everyone else that Daniel had chosen the correct course of action.

Daniel's decision is even more admirable when you consider that he was a young person. He didn't yield to the pressure to give in to what the other, older people wanted him to do. He worked out a compromise that allowed him to maintain his integrity (not a compromise of his beliefs, but a compromise of actions).

"But," you say, "sometimes you just can't compromise. Then what?" Then you need to examine the examples of Shadrach, Meshach, and Abednego. They knew where they had to draw the line. Even at risk of their lives, they chose to stand by their beliefs rather than compromise. And God honored their actions, just as He had honored Daniel's.

Now, how about *your* actions? When you feel peer pressure to do things that you really don't believe are right, how do you handle those situations? For each of the situations listed below, first establish whether you have to "draw the line"—decide that the situation is wrong, no matter what. Then try to think of a compromise you could work out to avoid totally breaking off your relationship with the person(s) putting pressure on you. A sample has been done for you.

THE SITUATION	WHERE WOULD YOU HAVE TO DRAW THE LINE?	COULD YOU COME UP WITH A COMPROMISE?
Your boss wants you to falsify some items on the annual report.	I would have to say no because I think lying is morally wrong.	I could explore some honest ways to report information.
Your closest friends are experimenting with drugs and want you to join them.		
You're at a party and offered a Scotch and soda in front of a lot of people you'd like to impress.		
You are told that you could join a prestigious country club if you would quit hanging around your "ethnic" friends so much.		
Your fiancé is pressuring you to have sex.		

What are some other situations where you feel pressure from other people to do things you don't think are right? What do you do in those situations?

At this point, it's important to keep in mind one other lesson from the life of Daniel. As Daniel, Shadrach, Meshach, and Abednego held up under pressure and didn't give in, and as God rewarded their stand, they began to have influence over everybody else. You can reach the point (if you develop confidence in yourself and in God's ability to get you through pressure situations) where *you* start exerting peer pressure on others.

Why not let your challenge for the next week be to make yourself such a positive influence on the people around you that they want to hear what you have to say about making hard decisions? Everyone is looking for answers to tough issues. If you can provide godly, workable answers for questions about sex, drugs, drinking, and all the other "pressure points" in life, you may discover that you have more friends than you ever would have expected.

KEY VERSE

"Praise be to the God of Shadrach, Meshach, and Abednego, who has sent His angel and rescued His servants! They trusted in Him and defied the king's command and were willing to give up their lives rather than serve or worship any god except their own God" (Daniel 3:28).

Jean and Sara may have a problem seeing things clearly.

8

OUT OF THE FUTURE, INTO THE LIONS' DEN
(Daniel 6—12)

Sara and Jean were having one of their regular gripe sessions. Today's topic: the injustices of the world—and more specifically, the easy life of Reginald Royalbody.

"It's just not fair!" exclaimed Jean. "Reggie has all that money while we have to scrimp and save just to get by."

"Sure, he has a law practice," added Sara. "But it's a cushy one in his father's firm. It just about makes me sick when I hear people talk about how hard he works. Who's he trying to impress anyway?"

"I have no idea," replied Jean. "With all his money, it's got to be an act. And you'd think he would get enough attention at work. But no! He makes it a point to be at our singles' group every week to try to impress us there."

Sara responded, "He sure goes out of his way to make sure he speaks to everyone and doesn't play favorites. And do you remember how he always volunteers his van for group trips? Just another way to flaunt his prestige, if you ask me. Even that mission trip he put together was just another way to get his name in the papers."

"Yeah, it was great to read about how our group went to Mexico and practically rebuilt a town after that earthquake hit. But when he was quoted saying he was insignificant and God should get all the glory, that really called attention to himself."

"He must think he's so good."

"Yeah."

"Yeah."

We'll leave Sara and Jean to their discussion. It's too bad Reginald didn't have an opportunity to defend himself, because it sounds like he has done some good things. Sara and Jean seem to resent the fact that Reginald has money, but they didn't exactly come up with many specific, valid reasons to put the guy down.

Maybe you've been a participant (or an eavesdropper) in a similar conversation. The next time you get the chance, listen closely and try to determine exactly whose ego is on the line. We don't know too much about Reginald's attitude. Maybe it could stand some improvement. But we know for sure that Jean and Sara have problems seeing things clearly. In their attempt to maintain a feeling of personal self-worth, they were trying to bring someone else's into question. In other words, it wasn't Reggie's ego that was a problem; it was Jean's and Sara's.

People with ego problems have lots of other problems as well. A faulty ego has a lot of negative by-products. Some of these other problems include jealousy, hypocrisy, greed, lack of forgiveness, and many others. In fact, you should observe several ego-related problems as you go through this session.

JOURNEY ONWARD

You may have noticed in the last session that the Book of Daniel seems different from the other prophetic books you've been through so far. The first half is full of personal stories and specific historic events. There are very few poetic passages or obscure predictions. But Daniel was every bit the prophet that Isaiah, Jeremiah, and Ezekiel were. In this session you will discover that he had his share of visions with complex, heavy-duty interpretations. But first, we'll begin with a story that you're probably familiar with.

Even though you've heard the story of Daniel in the lions' den dozens of times, read it again closely—as if this is the first time. Specifically, look at all the details in this account. It's full of emotions, motivations, and nitty-gritty description. Try not to miss any of it.

Read Daniel 6:1-28.
What caused Daniel to fall out of favor with the other Babylonian leaders? (Daniel 6:1-4)

Notice that the ego problem has already come into play. Based on all the events of the last session, who would be better than Daniel to oversee the kingdom? But that's not the way the other satraps saw it. (A group of provinces was called a satrapy, and their rulers were called satraps.) But even though they followed Daniel around, intentionally trying to find something for which they could accuse him, they were unable to do so. Finally, however, they came up with a way to get him. What did they do? (6:5-9)

How did Daniel react to the king's new command? (6:10)

Of course, the other satraps were spying on Daniel and couldn't wait to run to King Darius and squeal on him. How did the king respond when he discovered that Daniel had disobeyed the royal decree? (6:11-14)

Getting Personal — *Have you ever thought about disobeying the law because of religious convictions? Why or why not?*

But there was really nothing King Darius could do. He had been caught by a direct appeal to his ego, and now it was too late to change his previous command. He had no choice but to go ahead and throw Daniel into the lions' den, with a quick expression of hope that somehow Daniel's God would rescue him. (He apparently knew better than to hope the Babylonian gods could help Daniel in any way.) How did King Darius feel after his judgment on Daniel? (6:16-18)

We are told that the king got up "at the first light of dawn," rushed to the lions' den, and "called out to Daniel in an anguished voice" (6:19-20). He must not have had as much faith in Daniel's God as he had in the track record of the Babylonian lions in the den. What specific things did Daniel want King Darius to know right away? (6:21-22)

So Daniel was pulled out of the lions' den without even a wound (6:23). How do we know that the lions were really down there, or that they weren't just sick, or that maybe they just had an off night? (6:24)

Getting Personal — *Have you ever experienced the power of God's protection? What was the circumstance?*

As you can see, the Persians were a cruel people. But even their top leader had a deep respect for Daniel and Daniel's God. What did King Darius do to prove that he had been impressed by God's power to protect His people? (6:25-27)

To this point, the Book of Daniel has been chronological. But now it flashes back a bit. If you remember the order of kings in this book, there was first

Babylonian King Nebuchadnezzar, followed by Babylonian King Belshazzar, and then Persian King Darius. (By the way, this order of kings makes it clear that Daniel must not have been a youngster by the time he was thrown into the lions' den, as he is sometimes pictured.)

Daniel's Dreams
Read Daniel 7:1–8:27.
Chapters 7 and 8 of Daniel go back to the reign of King Belshazzar. But having already discussed the events of the kingdom, Daniel now wants to cover some dreams and visions he had. In the first year of Belshazzar's reign, Daniel had a dream about four beasts. Reread Daniel 7:1-8 and describe each beast below.

❏ BEAST #1

❏ BEAST #2

❏ BEAST #3

❏ BEAST #4

In contrast to these four beasts, Daniel saw a vision of God. (He refers to Him as the "Ancient of Days.") How did he describe God? (7:9-10)

Watchmen Who Wouldn't Quit

As Daniel continued to watch, he saw the first three beasts come and go, but the new horn of the fourth beast continued to issue boastful words until the fourth beast was also killed and its body thrown into a blazing fire (7:11-12). Then what did Daniel see? (7:13-14)

Who do you think this person with God was? Defend your answer.

As Daniel observed all this, he didn't respond much better than any of us would. He was troubled by what he saw, and he didn't understand any of it. But he wasn't afraid to ask. He approached one of the angels in his vision to get an explanation. What did the angel explain was the interpretation of the four beasts? (7:15-18)

What was the interpretation of the fourth beast and its horns? (7:23-25)

You may notice that the angel's interpretation of Daniel's vision is much like Daniel's interpretation of King Nebuchadnezzar's dream about the large statue with the head of gold and feet of iron mixed with clay (Daniel 2). Both visions used symbols of four kingdoms (later identified as Babylon, Medo-Persia, Greece, and Rome). And in both cases, the four major nations are followed by the coming of God's kingdom.

A couple of years later, Daniel had another major vision. What did he see this time? (8:1-12)

Again, the interpretation immediately follows the vision. And this is one of the few places in the Bible where a heavenly being is called by name. What was the name of the angel who interpreted Daniel's vision for him? (8:15-16)

The ram in Daniel's vision represented the Medo-Persian Empire. The goat symbolized Greece. And in retrospect, we know that the "horn" (v. 9) was the symbol for a Greek king named Antiochus IV Epiphanes who desecrated the Jewish temple and persecuted the Jews in 167 B.C. After seeing this vision, how did Daniel respond? (8:27)

Read Daniel 9:1-19.
Daniel had been through a lot in his lifetime. As a young man, he was carried away from his homeland into Babylon. He served well under Nebuchadnezzar and Belshazzar, until the Medes and Persians overpowered the Babylonians. Then he faithfully served King Darius, the Mede. And through all this, he remained true to God. He not only prayed regularly, but he also read the Scriptures that were available in his time. One day he was reading what Jeremiah had written and discovered that the Jewish exile was to last 70 years. This discovery led him to pray for his people (9:1-19). And as he was praying, he was again visited by the Angel Gabriel.

Seventy Sevens
Read Daniel 9:20-27.
Gabriel gave Daniel a specific revelation, though you need to read it carefully to understand it. (And you may need to pull out a calculator to make sense of it.) Gabriel foretold a period of time consisting of "seventy 'sevens'" (9:24). The "sevens" refer to periods of seven years each, so the "seventy 'sevens'" would be 70 x 7 years, or 490 years.

But there was a catch. Only 69 of the "sevens" (or 483 years) would take place between the rebuilding of Jerusalem and the time that the "Anointed One" (Jesus) would come to His people and be killed. And while some people disagree, many Bible scholars believe that there is an undetermined time lapse between the end of the 69th "seven" and the beginning of the

70th "seven." (Confused yet? If so, just go slowly and reread Daniel 9:20-27. It's not as complicated as it sounds.)

During the last "seven," according to Gabriel, a ruler will make a covenant with the Jewish people. But halfway through the period he will break the treaty and desecrate the temple (9:27). And note that this event is in the context of "the end," with war and desolation rampant. Many people believe this period to be the rule of the one called the Antichrist—just prior to Jesus' return to Earth. But Gabriel was sure to emphasize that this figure will rule only "until the end that is decreed is poured out on him" (9:27). Even during times when ungodly people think they are being victorious, God is in control.

Read Daniel 10:1-21.
The rest of the Book of Daniel takes place during the reign of Cyrus. You should remember that he was the Persian king who allowed Ezra to take the Jews back to Jerusalem to rebuild the temple (Ezra 1). But even as Daniel was seeing many of his people return to their homeland, he received a revelation of a great war. What effect did this vision have on him? (10:1-3)

So a heavenly visitor was sent to Daniel to explain to him the things that would come to pass. Describe the person whom Daniel saw (10:4-6).

No one besides Daniel could see the heavenly being, and even Daniel was weak in his presence. Why had it taken three weeks for the heavenly being to get to Daniel with an answer to his questions? (10:10-14)

[The "prince of the Persian kingdom" was apparently a supernatural being who fought for Satan. Michael is one of the chief angels who serves God.]

But after Daniel's visitor finally got there, he strengthened Daniel to prepare him for the news to come (10:18-19). He had come to tell Daniel what was

Out of the Future, Into the Lions' Den

written in the "Book of Truth" (10:20-21). We don't know exactly what this Book was, but it was apparently some kind of heavenly record of truth, wisdom, and knowledge.

Read Daniel 11:1-45.
The angel first told Daniel about specific events to occur in the near future. The description in Daniel 11:1-35 supports Daniel's previous visions: kings of Persia (v. 2) would be followed by a Greek empire headed by "a mighty king" (v. 3). This king was apparently Alexander the Great. All the events recorded in this section of Daniel have specific historic parallels. But the rest of the chapter describes a future time. What kind of person will be ruling during this time? (11:36-45)

The "king" mentioned in this passage is another reference to the Antichrist. Notice again that Daniel is told that this figure "will come to his end, and no one will help him" (11:45).

Read Daniel 12:1-13.
What are some specific events that will take place during the last days, during and after the rule of the Antichrist? (12:1-3)

Daniel was instructed to seal up what he had been told, because there was no way for his people to understand anything close to all he had been told. But looking back through history, we can see that his prophecies concerning the Medo-Persian, Greek, and Roman Empires were amazingly accurate. So we have no reason to question the accuracy of his visions concerning future events. Even though these are hard things to understand, it is important that we make every effort to comprehend them. The first thing we need to do is try to remain close to God. Why? (12:8-10)

The image of Daniel in this session is quite different from what you saw in the last session. Most of us know Daniel from the popular Bible stories. But his dreams and visions were as specific and as noteworthy as any other prophet's. And it's comforting to realize that the same God who delivered him from the den of lions is the One who gave him clear insight into his future—and ours.

JOURNEY INWARD

The Book of Daniel provides a good context for examining the subject of *ego*. In the last session, you saw how Babylonian kings Nebuchadnezzar and Belshazzar had to suffer because of their false pride. And in this session, the egocentric plans of the Persian leaders put Daniel in the lions' den for a night, but backfired and eventually consumed them all—literally. As we look into the future and see the image of the coming Antichrist, he too is characterized by boasting and pride.

So think for a few moments about ways *your* ego may cause problems for you and those around you. Answer the following questions as honestly and as specifically as possible.

❑ How does your jealousy of others get in the way of building strong relationships with them?

❑ What talents or accomplishments do you have that you are proud of? Is there a possibility that you may be a little *too* proud about one or more of these things?

❑ Do you spend more time worrying about how *you* can be important, or can you relax because you know God has all the important (and seemingly unimportant) things under control?

Now focus on one of the areas where you could stand some improvement and come up with a plan to get your ego out of the way. Then do whatever it takes to put your plan into action. And come back frequently to the Book of Daniel. It's hard to imagine what kind of discipline it must have taken for him to see the things he saw and still be so servant-minded to the foreign kings who asked for his help. But Daniel knew who was calling the shots—and it wasn't Daniel!

Daniel didn't boast or brag. He didn't complain about his hardships. He didn't alter his spiritual commitments in the least to try to get others to like and accept him. He just lived his life for God, whether that meant recording secret mysteries of the heavenly kingdom, observing visions of the future, or sitting alone in a den of hungry lions. And he showed us that God can do big things for people with small egos. Daniel set an example we all need to follow.

KEY VERSES

"He is the living God and He endures forever; His kingdom will not be destroyed, His dominion will never end. He rescues and He saves; He performs signs and wonders in the heavens and on the earth" (Daniel 6:26-27).

*What image comes to mind when you hear the word **faithful**?*

9

LOUSY IS THY FAITHFULNESS

(Hosea, Joel, Amos)

The following definitions all pertain to the same word. See how quickly you can guess what the word is.

DEFINITION #1: "Given with strong assurance."

DEFINITION #2: "True to the facts, to a standard, or to an original."

DEFINITION #3: "Firm in adherence to promises or duties."

DEFINITION #4: "Steadfast in affection or allegiance."

DEFINITION #5: "Full of faith."

BONUS CLUE FOR THE EXCEPTIONALLY SLOW: A variation of the word is used in the title of this session.

How many clues did it take you to discover that the word was *faithful*? You don't hear too much about faithfulness these days. And when you do, it's not often in connection with people. You might think of Yellowstone Park's "Old Faithful" geyser, that faithfully spouts water into the air every 65 minutes or so. Or a "faithful" pet might come to mind. One of the last truly faithful people was the Lone Ranger's "faithful" Indian companion, Tonto.

Perhaps you don't hear too much about faithfulness because it's not a short-term trait. Faithfulness must be proven again and again over a long period of time. It takes a number of years for someone to prove to be a faithful parent, faithful spouse, or faithful child. When all is said and done, few people truly qualify for the honor of being called faithful.

And because faithfulness is difficult, some people don't even try to be faithful. It's much easier to always do what seems best for yourself instead of showing faithfulness to others. Yet a lifestyle that focuses on self will always cause problems. And even more serious problems arise in a spiritual context when God expects our faithfulness and we aren't accustomed to being faithful to anyone.

JOURNEY ONWARD

The next four sessions will have much to say about faithfulness as we go into the books of the "minor prophets." The adjective *minor* shouldn't imply that these 12 people were any less important than Isaiah, Jeremiah, Ezekiel, and Daniel. But their writings are much shorter, so they don't often get top billing. Yet you will soon see that these men provided several prophecies that are found nowhere else. And there are some very special people and familiar stories from these books.

So don't be reluctant to go through these books, even if it *is* the first time you've tried to care about people like Obadiah, Habakkuk, and Zephaniah. In fact, you'll be going through three books in each of the next four sessions; so, far from being bored, you may find yourself struggling to keep up with what all these guys have to say.

Read Hosea 1:1-11.
The first writer is one of the most unusual of the minor prophets—Hosea. He lived and prophesied in the final years before Israel's fall at the hands of the Assyrians (before their captivity). And perhaps the importance of faithfulness made a bigger impact on him than any of the other prophets. Why? (Hosea 1:1-3)

This is probably one of the strangest commands of God recorded in the Bible, and interpreters aren't sure whether Gomer was a prostitute before she

Lousy Is Thy Faithfulness

married Hosea or if she became unfaithful after her marriage. (The grammatical tense in the original language allows for either translation.) Likewise, the phrase "children of unfaithfulness" doesn't necessarily mean that Hosea wasn't their real father. Hosea could be the father, but Gomer's marital infidelity would cause her kids to be "children of unfaithfulness."

Hosea and Gomer eventually had three children, and their names were symbolic. Hosea's name meant "salvation," but his kids' names were quite different. One of the names meant "not my people," another meant "God scatters," and the third meant "not loved." Reread Hosea 1:4-9. Record the names of Hosea's children. Then notice what God had to say about each name and see if you can match the name with its correct English translation.

Read Hosea 2:1-23.
It doesn't take long to see that God was allowing Hosea to experience firsthand what it was like to have an unfaithful wife who cared more about others than her true husband. Gomer's *literal* adultery was a clear (though painful) object lesson to illustrate the *spiritual* adultery of Israel and Judah. God's relationship to His people was often symbolized by marriage in the Old Testament (and New Testament, as well). Using this parallel, how does God plan to get His sinful "wife" to return to Him? (2:2-7)

Getting Personal — *Have you ever had an unfaithful friend? Were you able to reconcile? Why or why not?*

How could Israel expect to be treated when they finally decided to return to God? (2:14-16, 23)

Read Hosea 3:1-5.
How did God have Hosea illustrate God's undying love for His people? (3:1-3)

Read Hosea 4:1-19.
The rest of the Book of Hosea deals with the specific sins of Israel, the judgment they could expect from God if they didn't repent, and their eventual restoration to God's good graces. And though these chapters are more prophetic than personal, the theme of faithfulness (or lack of it) continues. In fact, what was God's main complaint about Israel? (4:1-2)

What was at the root of Israel's unfaithfulness? (4:10)

Getting Personal — *What is at the root of your unfaithfulness?*

Skim Hosea 5:1–10:15.
The Israelites were still claiming to follow God at this time, but what might indicate that their claims were shallow, if not completely false? (8:2-6)

What was to happen to them as a result? (8:7-10)

Read Hosea 11:1-12.
Hosea 11 contains a clear statement of God's love for His people. This time He speaks of Israel as His child rather than His wife, and reminds them of all the things He had done for them while they were "growing up." And while Israelite law provided for death by stoning of a stubborn, unrepentant child (Deuteronomy 21:18-21), God loved His rebellious people too much to destroy them completely. In this context, the captivity of Israel seems like a compassionate judgment, no matter how unpleasant it was for the people. Specifically, what things had God done to prove that He loved His people? (11:1-4)

Skim Hosea 12:1–14:9.
What was God's final message to Israel through Hosea? (14:1-2, 9)

Joel
Read Joel 1:1-20.
The Book of Hosea is followed in the Bible by the Book of Joel. Not too much is known about Joel. He doesn't record where he lived, when he did his prophesying, or any events of his lifetime that would help establish a historical context. He and his father, Pethuel, aren't listed in any of the biblical genealogies. Yet Joel spoke with the authority of God as he wrote of a specific judgment to come upon Judah—a plague of invading locusts that would hit the land. How severe would the locust plague be? (Joel 1:1-4)

To what did Joel compare the locust invasion? (1:5-7)

Exactly how were the locusts going to disrupt the people of Judah? (1:8-12)

Joel left no doubt that the locusts were connected with God's judgment on the people of Judah (1:15). But the people of Judah weren't the only ones to be affected by the nasty insects. What other creatures would suffer because of them? (1:18-20)

Read Joel 2:1-32.
The second chapter of Joel continues with the theme of an invading army, and again there is some debate among interpreters as to whether Joel was continuing his locust description or if he subtly moved into a description of an actual army for which he uses the analogy of locusts. Reread 2:1-11. How might these verses be a good description for invading locusts?

How might the same verses accurately describe an invading army of human beings?

Regardless of whether the invaders were to be insects or humans, what did God want the people of Judah to do? (2:12-13)

What did God promise to do if the people responded to Him? (2:18-20, 24-27)

Joel then relayed a prophecy of God that was recalled hundreds of years later, even after Jesus had come to earth, died, risen from the dead, and ascended back into heaven. What did Joel predict would happen? (2:28-32)

When did this prophecy partially come to pass? (Acts 2:1-4, 14-21)

Read Joel 3:1-21.
The ultimate fulfillment of Joel's prophecy is yet to occur, when God will completely destroy the enemies of His people. The mention of how "the sun will be turned to darkness and the moon to blood" (Joel 2:31) suggests that these events will be a result of warfare. What else does Joel say that supports that idea? (3:9-16)

Knowing of the big battle that will take place in the last days, in what can God's people find assurance? (3:17-21)

Amos
Skim Amos 1:1–7:17.
A third prophet who brought a similar message of Israel's coming judgment (and eventual forgiveness) is Amos. Hosea and Joel had prophesied that God's judgment would be certain, but had focused much of their attention on the restoration of their nation. Amos, however, was much more emphatic about the severity of the bad times to come. His writings end on an optimistic note, but the bulk of his book is centered on the dim future of Israel prior to their return from captivity.

Amos didn't hold a priestly or a particularly "spiritual" job before he was a prophet. What did he do for a living? (Amos 1:1; 7:14)

Amos prophesied during the reign of Judah's King Uzziah, so he lived at about the same time as Isaiah, Hosea, and Jonah (whom we will examine in the next session). During that time, the people of Israel felt pretty safe and sound from its enemies, and they were drifting away from a closeness to God that Elisha had struggled to establish a few years before. So Amos had the job of focusing their attention on their weak worship habits. As he began his writing, Amos didn't say, "Uh, I have a message from God if, uh, I could have your attention." How did he let the people know God wanted to speak to them? (1:2)

He first recited specific charges against Israel's enemies (1:3-8), then their allies (1:9–2:3), and finally Israel and Judah themselves (2:4-16). What were some of the things for which God was holding Israel and Judah accountable? (2:4-8)

Getting Personal — *What is God holding you accountable for?*

What did Amos tell the people to expect? (3:7, 11-12)

Much of their improper behavior was of a social nature. What social practices did God want the Israelites to correct? (5:11-15)

Other of their offenses were of a religious nature. What religious practices did God want the Israelites to correct? (5:18-24)

Why had the Israelites become so unfeeling? (6:1, 4-7)

God showed Amos two things that He could have done to bring judgment on the Israelites, but Amos interceded and God didn't send those harsh judgments. What were the first two potential judgments that Amos saw? (7:1-6)

But God wanted Amos to see that the Israelites were "out of kilter," so to speak. So Amos saw a vision of God holding a plumb line (a string with a weight at one end). During Amos' time, a builder used a plumb line when putting up walls to insure that they were straight. Then later on, the walls would be tested again to see if they had shifted while settling and needed to be torn down. God wanted Amos to see that Israel had at one time been "straight and true" but had gradually gotten to the stage where it needed major repair. And this time God didn't pause long enough to let Amos object (7:7-9).

It's not surprising that as Amos passed along God's words to the people, he encountered opposition. What problem did he face in Israel? (7:10-13)

What personal prophecy did Amos have for his pain-in-the-neck counterpart? (7:14-17)

Watchmen Who Wouldn't Quit

What prophecy did Amos emphasize concerning Israel? (7:17)

Read Amos 8:1–9:15.
Amos then saw another vision. What was it, and what did it mean? (8:1-2)

What truly dreadful suffering was God going to allow His people to experience? (8:11-12)

Getting Personal – *What kind of suffering has God allowed you to experience? Why?*

In Amos' final recorded vision, he saw God poised and ready to bring judgment on Israel—beginning at the temple (9:1). Amos told the people that they would have no place to hide from God's judgment—that is, if they remained defiant to God (9:2-4). How extensive would God's judgment be? (9:8-10)

But after the nation went through the severe judgment of God, what could they look forward to? (9:11-15)

JOURNEY INWARD

As you have seen, the minor prophets make several noteworthy observations concerning **faithfulness**. And if you were looking closely, you probably noticed that faithfulness needs to work on a couple of different levels.

The first basic level of faithfulness is one that is personal and practical. For instance, when Hosea married Gomer, he expected her to be faithful to him in return for his faithfulness to her. Marriage is only one of the commitments people make in which a certain level of faithfulness is expected. Others include family relationships, business agreements, team sports, and friendships, to name a few. In each of these areas, your faithfulness to the other person(s) involved should be more important than your *own* wants.

Hosea and his three children all had to suffer because Gomer decided to do what she wanted to do rather than be faithful to her husband and family. Think of the people to whom you should be faithful. List them below in the first column. Then in the second column, think of a time when you were unfaithful to that person (or when you thought about being unfaithful). Describe how your relationship with each person suffered (or could have suffered) because of your unfaithfulness.

PERSONS TO WHOM I HAVE A COMMITMENT TO BE FAITHFUL	WHAT MIGHT HAPPEN IF I DECIDE NOT TO BE FAITHFUL TO THIS PERSON

A second and even deeper level of faithfulness is of a spiritual nature. Hosea's painful experience with personal unfaithfulness made him very aware of his people's spiritual unfaithfulness to God. His concerns were echoed by Joel and Amos. All of these prophets knew that God's faithfulness to His people was not being returned. And they knew that since the people refused to honor their commitment to worship God alone, God was going to allow them to suffer until they again became faithful to Him.

We all have obligations to be faithful to God in certain areas. Some of our commitments are commanded in the Bible (prayer, Bible study, and so forth). Others are things we have promised to do (early morning quiet times, hospital visitation, missions projects and other church-related activities, etc.). Whenever we fail to honor our commitments to God, *we* are the ones who usually suffer for our unfaithfulness. (No, God doesn't reach for the nearest lightning bolt and hurl it in our direction; we suffer because God knows what is best for us. So when we disobey, we settle for less than the best.)

On the following chart, first list the specific things you know you should be doing out of your faithfulness to God. In the second column, list the ways you may have to suffer if you neglect to remain faithful in any of those activities.

ACTIVITIES BY WHICH I SHOW MY FAITHFULNESS TO GOD	WHAT MIGHT HAPPEN IF I DECIDE NOT TO BE FAITHFUL IN THIS AREA

Lousy Is Thy Faithfulness

A favorite hymn of many people is titled, "Great Is Thy Faithfulness." And it should go without saying that when God promises to do something, it will certainly come to pass. But as we stand in church and sing, "Great Is Thy Faithfulness," we need to ask ourselves what God thinks about *our* faithfulness. Can you call your level of faithfulness "Great"? "Pretty good"? "Average"? "Lousy"?

To close, review your two charts and locate any areas that reflect a weakness in your level of faithfulness. (It will probably help to begin with your faithfulness to God and then go back and review your faithfulness to others.) Confess any shortcomings that have come to light and ask God for strength for the future. You may want to recommit yourself to anything you know you should be doing, but aren't.

After you mend any weak relationships between you and God, do the same thing for other people. If you sense a possible conflict between yourself and anyone else, do what you can to correct the situation. If it's too late to prevent a problem, try to restore your tense or broken relationships.

Faithfulness is more than just a characteristic of "nice" people. It is a requirement for godly living and a good Christian lifestyle. The Israelites drifted away from God so gradually that they still thought they were being faithful. We must avoid the same mistake. So review the definitions at the beginning of this session. If any one of them is untrue about your relationship with God, make it your goal for this week to faithfully work out the problem.

KEY VERSE

"Rend your heart and not your garments. Return to the Lord your God, for He is gracious and compassionate, slow to anger and abounding in love, and He relents from sending calamity" (Joel 2:13).

How safe do you feel?

10

UNSAFE AND SECURE
(Obadiah, Jonah, Micah)

Imagine yourself in each of the following situations. After each one, record whether you would feel more secure or less secure after the action taken by the other person in the illustration.

Situation #1—You've just flown into New York City to visit a friend. You're taking a taxi from the airport to the person's apartment, and you notice that you're going through a neighborhood that definitely would never make the cover of *Better Homes and Gardens*. The taxi driver notices your worried look, bends over to push a button, and the doors automatically lock. Do you feel more secure or less secure? Why?

Situation #2—You're looking for a new place for your family to live. You find a home you all really like, but you notice the door lock is missing. When you point it out to the real estate agent, she says, "Don't worry. Some of the local gangs broke in the other day and caused some damage. But it's taken care of now, and we're going to install *three* locks on the door before you move in." Do you feel more secure or less secure? Why?

Situation #3—You've just taken a job in a convenience store. Your new boss is telling you that recently in a store (just like yours) across town, the owner was robbed at gunpoint. But your boss says, "Don't worry. We carry a special kind of 'insurance' here," and reaches down to pull out a gun of his own. Do you feel more secure or less secure? Why?

It's not too hard to define security, but it's harder to identify just what makes us feel secure or insecure. As infants, we get by with parents and teddy bears (or security blankets, or sucking our thumbs, or any number of things). But as we get older and see more of the world as it really is, our sense of security is threatened. And since we've outgrown teddy bears, we look for security in other things—guns, locks, insurance policies, bank vaults, karate classes, or whatever. The problem is, we can take steps to protect ourselves and our belongings, but the *feeling* of security doesn't always accompany our actions.

For each of the situations above, the very fact that the other person was taking steps to address a problem was proof that the problem must be pretty bad. It wasn't a bad idea for the person to "play it safe," but the underlying feeling was that you'd better watch out for anything that could possibly go wrong. And how can you ever feel secure when you're watching out all the time?

JOURNEY ONWARD

This session will introduce you to three more of the minor prophets, and each of these three people will teach you something about security. As you read what they have to say, try to see what made them secure. At the end of the session, you'll have an opportunity to evaluate your attitudes toward the things that make you secure (or insecure).

The first guy who has something to say is Obadiah, but he doesn't say all that much. In fact, he provides only 21 verses' worth of content. (His is the shortest book in the Old Testament.) Yet what he says about security (or false security, to be more exact) is very significant.

Obadiah's prophecy focuses on the Edomites, who were gloating over Judah's

Unsafe and Secure

suffering. (The Edomites were the descendants of Esau, while the Israelites—and Judahites—were the descendants of his tricky twin brother, Jacob. Tension and conflict had existed between these peoples for most of their existence.) The exact instance that caused Judah's problems and Obadiah's observations is unclear, but it was possibly the nation's conquest by the Babylonians.

Read Obadiah 1-21.
Obadiah's vision was a message from God to Edom. What attitude did God see in the Edomites? (Obadiah 3-4)

Because of their callous attitude, what was going to happen to the Edomites? (6-10)

How did God feel about the fact that Edom had received great satisfaction by seeing their neighbors (the people of Judah) suffer? (11-16)

Getting Personal — *Have you ever felt happy when one of your enemies experienced some form of suffering? How do you think God feels about your attitude?*

Judah was down, at least temporarily. Were they ready to be "counted out"? Explain your answer. (17-18, 21)

Obadiah shows us that it's improper to celebrate the sufferings of others—even enemies. We shouldn't attempt to find security for ourselves at the expense of others. The next prophet teaches some additional lessons about security.

Jonah
Read Jonah 1:1-17.
You probably know a lot about this guy already, but you may not know the end of his story. When it came to being a good prophet of God, how secure was Jonah? (Jonah 1:1-3)

If you don't have a Bible atlas handy, you may not realize how hard Jonah tried to avoid following God's instructions. Nineveh was several hundred miles northeast of Israel/Judah, and Tarshish is thought to be in what is now Spain (about 2,500 miles *west*). With such a strong desire to disobey God, what kept Jonah from getting to Tarshish? (1:4)

While the sailors were sweating it out on deck and throwing good cargo overboard for safety's sake, what was Jonah doing? (1:5)

After the pagan sea captain scolded the undercover prophet of God for not praying, the sailors decided to cast lots to see if they could discover exactly who was the cause of all their trouble. And sure enough, the lot fell on Jonah. What attitude did they have toward him? Why? (1:7-13)

It's somewhat surprising that Jonah comes across as such a weakling and bad guy, while the sailors seem to be likeable and compassionate. But finally, at Jonah's command, they reluctantly tossed him overboard. You probably know that God sent a great fish to swallow Jonah. What two other events took place as soon as Jonah hit the water? (1:15-16)

How long was Jonah inside the fish? (1:17)

Unsafe and Secure

Read Jonah 2:1-10.
While he was in the fish, Jonah figured it might be a good idea to pray. You would think that his prayer would be one of desperation and insecurity. But for someone who was living underwater for 72 hours without coming up for air, Jonah sounded pretty secure. Review his prayer and jot down phrases that indicate his level of security (2:1-9).

Getting Personal – *How secure in God are you?*

After Jonah had decided that preaching to the Ninevites might be preferable to becoming a permanent part of a fish's digestive system, what happened to him? (2:10)

Read Jonah 3:1-10.
Why do you think Jonah might have been reluctant to go to Nineveh in the first place? (3:1-3)

Getting Personal – *Have you ever resisted God's calling? Why or why not?*

Jonah doesn't tell us too much about the specific wrongdoings of Nineveh, but Nahum will spell out several of them in the next session. You might think that the capital city of the greatest nation on earth would feel pretty secure about their ability to defend themselves in any emergency. Yet how did the Ninevites respond to Jonah's prophecy from God? (3:5-9)

How did God respond when He saw the repentance of the Ninevites? (3:10)

Read Jonah 4:1-11.
How did *Jonah* respond when he saw the repentance of the Ninevites? (4:1-3)

It would have been so neat and convenient if the story of Jonah had ended with the great spiritual revival in Nineveh. But the Bible is brutally honest in recording the foibles and weaknesses of God's people. Jonah is one of the best examples. He had the nerve to stand there and be angry at God because God didn't wipe out a metropolis before his eyes. (Sure, the Assyrians were major enemies of Israel, but you'd think that Jonah—of all people—would be especially glad for God's willingness to offer a second chance to disobedient men and women.) Since God didn't answer Jonah's request to take his life, Jonah decided to stake out the city "just in case" something exciting happened. What did God do that pleased Jonah? (4:5-6)

But what happened to change Jonah's attitude? (4:7-8)

What did God want Jonah to learn? (4:9-11)

Jonah's account goes rather well with Obadiah's story. While Obadiah taught that Israel's enemies shouldn't rejoice in Judah's suffering, God showed Jonah that it was wrong for Judah to rejoice in the fall of *their* enemies, if those enemies were willing to repent instead. Lest we be too hard on Jonah, we need to keep in mind that with all the political activity in the world in Jonah's day, it was natural for God's people to be fiercely loyal to their own country. In most cases, they would assume that God didn't want any of the ungodly nations to rule over them. But God made it clear to Jonah that He would rather see wicked people repent than be destroyed.

Micah

The third and final prophet of this session is Micah. He prophesied at about the same time as Isaiah and Hosea—before the Israelites had gone into captivity. And like so many of the other prophets we've already seen, Micah brought a message mixed with both the certainty of the coming judgment of God and the deliverance that would follow. In addition, Micah provides us some information that no other prophet duplicates.

Read Micah 1:1-16.
What places in Israel did Micah specifically single out to receive the judgment of God? (Micah 1:3-5)

What would happen to these places? (1:6-7)

What would be the means by which God would execute His judgment? (1:15-16)

Read Micah 2:1-13.
Like Amos, Micah cited certain social sins of which the people were guilty. What were some of his specific charges? (2:1-2, 8-11)

But even though Micah was clear about the sins of Israel and the captivity to come, what promise did he bring from God? (2:12-13)

Read Micah 3:1-12.
What was the difference between the false prophets of Israel and God's true prophet, Micah? (3:4-8)

Read Micah 4:1-13.
Micah also wrote of "the last days" when Israel would be restored to prominence (4:1). It would be a time of spiritual renewal (4:2), peace (4:3), and prosperity (4:4). But in contrast to that scene, Micah paints a verbal picture of the exile that must come first. How did he describe Judah's period of exile? (4:10)

Read Micah 5:1-15.
And like Obadiah, Micah warned Israel's enemies of gloating over Israel's suffering. As bad as the situation must have looked to others, Micah assured them that it was part of God's plan to restore His people to good favor (4:11-13). Then Micah prophesied a future leader of Israel and the place that the leader would be born. What place did Micah name, and based on that information, which leader do you think he was referring to? (5:2)

Even though Israel was to "be abandoned" until this leader arrived (5:3), what would happen after this leader came? (5:4-9)

At that time, what things would God remove to ensure that His people depend only on Him? (5:10-15)

Skim Micah 6:1–7:20.
Micah then described a courtroom scene in which God first defends His actions by reminding the people of many of the things He had done for them during their history (6:1-5). Then He brings His charges against the people (6:9-16). What was it specifically that God wanted from His people? (6:8)

Unsafe and Secure

To close, Micah again summarized the wicked state of his people and his nation (7:1-6). Had he given up hope? (7:7-9)

After everything Micah had prophesied, what was on his mind as he closed his writings? (7:18-20)

JOURNEY INWARD

Now that you're halfway through the Minor Prophets, you may have noticed that their messages aren't minor at all. Sure, there's some repetition, which is to be expected due to the severe nature of the people's sin. But the tone of each book is a little different, and each writer offers new bits of information not available in the other books. As we did earlier in this session, we now want to focus our thoughts on the topic of **security**.

There are many kinds of false security. Obadiah had to get on the cases of the Edomites because they were feeling secure as a result of their enemy's disaster. Jonah looked for security by attempting to avoid challenging situations that might be uncomfortable or dangerous. The sailors on Jonah's ship looked for security in their gods. And Micah recorded a coming time when God would take away His people's horses, chariots, strongholds, witchcraft, and idols. Without any of the things they had previously used as "security blankets," the people would finally be able to find security in God alone.

Today we may not count too heavily on chariots or fortresses for security, but most of us probably have certain things that we use to help us feel more secure. Go through the list of items/people on page 134. Put a check mark (√) beside each thing that provides you with some kind of security. Then explain to what extent you are dependent on that item or person.

Watchmen Who Wouldn't Quit

- ❏ Locks (on cars, doors, bicycles, etc.)

- ❏ Insurance policies

- ❏ Stuffed animals (or similar childhood "security blankets")

- ❏ Spouse

- ❏ Brothers/Sisters

- ❏ Friends

- ❏ Money

- ❏ Possessions

- ❏ Intelligence, talent, or physical ability

- ❏ Status or social position

- ❏ Job

- ❏ Other_____

Unsafe and Secure

Locked doors, insurance policies, and security systems are fine, but none of these things are adequate replacements for a solid dependence on God. We need to remember that as we search for security for ourselves and our belongings, we fool ourselves if we don't leave everything in God's hands. Any security without God is false security.

Jonah learned the hard way. He used his money to head in the opposite direction from where God had told him to go. He probably thought he was going to pull it off. He was sleeping in the false security of his "escape from Nineveh" when he had a rude awakening. Before long he found himself tossed overboard to an almost certain death. But in the stomach of a large fish Jonah learned what real security is. God first took care of Jonah, and then Jonah was able to function effectively for God.

Review your comments concerning your sources of security. If any of them are getting in the way of a trusting relationship with God, you may need to let go of them for a while and see what God can do for you. Do you remember as a child when one of your parents would toss you up in the air and then catch you? You probably loved to fly through the air, sensing a little bit of danger, but with the assurance that your parent wouldn't let you get hurt. That's the kind of security God offers. You won't always *feel* safe and secure, but you can be assured of security even when you don't sense it. And with that element of freedom and adventure, doesn't life sound like a lot more fun? Try it and see.

KEY VERSES

"Who is a God like You, who pardons sin and forgives the transgression of the remnant of His inheritance? You do not stay angry forever but delight to show mercy. You will again have compassion on us; You will tread our sins underfoot and hurl all our iniquities into the depths of the sea" (Micah 7:18-19).

*According to the evidence, you're all guilty,
but I think I'll just let everybody go.*

11

WHAT'S YOUR VERDICT?
(Nahum, Habakkuk, Zephaniah)

"All rise! First Superior Court of Cannon County is now in session. Judge E.Z. Gooden presiding."

"Be seated. Bailiff, call the first case."

"Your honor, the defendant in this case has admitted to stealing his neighbor's Porsche, driving it around town at speeds in excess of 90 mph, endangering the lives of several women and small children, and finally plowing it into an empty shed. Damages amount to $37,659 . . . and 31 cents."

"Well, well, well. What a reckless young man. But I'll let him off the hook this time. Next case."

"Uh, yes, your honor. This young woman is accused of selling drugs to grammar school kids. We have affidavits from 16 witnesses, and when we searched her apartment we discovered large quantities of heroin, cocaine, and assorted pills. We have more than enough evidence for an unshakeable conviction."

"What do you have to say for yourself, young lady?"

"I needed the money. My clothes bills have just been out of sight lately. It's not like those little kids *had* to buy drugs from me. And, like, I'm really sorry (that I got caught)."

137

"Well, since you're sorry, I don't see that the court needs to be too strict. I'll let you off with the warning to not do this again. Next case!"

"Let's see. We have a child molester . . . with three previous convictions."

"Let him go. You can't believe the testimony of every kid who's covered with cuts and bruises."

"We also have a psycho killer, two rapists, some kidnappers, and a gang of kids who go around stealing kittens and puppies and offering them to Satan."

"Well, according to the evidence, they're all guilty. But hey, I'm a nice guy and I don't want anyone to think otherwise. So just let everybody go."

. . . .

If a judge ever took the attitude of the one just described, he would be disbarred and arrested (if not lynched!) before his gavel could hit the floor. No one would tolerate his atrocious disregard for the law. His job is to administer justice, and if he refused to do so, he wouldn't be respected by anyone.

Yet some people skim through the Old Testament and hurl all sorts of accusations at God about how He can't possibly be loving and forgiving. They assume that since God allowed His people to go into captivity and passed judgment on sinful nations, He must be unfeeling. They want a God who is all love and warmth, with no sense of justice and judgment. But it's clear that such a "judge" would not be tolerated—much less respected— by others.

God is the perfect example of love and forgiveness. And it is exactly because He loves His people that He cannot allow them to go on forever harming themselves and others without some kind of chastisement or judgment (just like a loving parent sometimes needs to reprimand a child who continually misbehaves). The prophets were called to bring this fact to people's attention, and in this session you will meet three more men who confronted their peers with the coming judgment of God.

What's Your Verdict?

JOURNEY ONWARD

The first writer, Nahum, gives us a sequel to Jonah's book. If Hollywood were doing his story, the title would be Jonah II, Return to Nineveh, Assyria Serial, or something similar. Very little is known about Nahum except the meaning of his name ("comfort") and his hometown (Elkosh—though no one is sure where this town was). His name was significant, since his message concerning Nineveh would bring comfort to Judah.

Nineveh had been around for quite a while. In fact, it was mentioned way back in Genesis 10:11-12. As capital of Assyria, Nineveh had become a powerful city. And the Ninevites maintained their power by showing no mercy in their battles. Records written by Nineveh's leaders speak of invading various areas and building pyramids out of the heads of people who had been conquered, of burning young men and maidens in the fire, of skinning defeated leaders and exhibiting the skin on the wall of the city, of cutting throats, cutting off hands, and much more. (Is it any wonder Jonah didn't want to go tell them to repent? It would be kind of like your going up to a vicious gang and telling them to change their violent ways or else.)

Yet the Ninevites *had* repented after Jonah's message. But their repentance was short-lived. It didn't take long for Nineveh to return to its brutal, wicked ways. As Nahum speaks of the city, it is not another call to repent. Rather, it is a stern and forceful description of judgment to come. Even though Assyria had already destroyed Samaria and taken the Israelites into captivity, Nahum spoke boldly of Nineveh's certain destruction.

Read Nahum 1:1-15.
How did Nahum deal with God's nature in regard to His judgment? In other words, did God's judgment on Nineveh mean that He was no longer a good and loving God? (Nahum 1:2-3, 7-8)

Getting Personal — *Have there been times in your life when you thought God was no longer good and loving? What were the circumstances? Did your attitude change? Why or why not?*

Watchmen Who Wouldn't Quit

Assyria was accustomed to being victorious in all its battles. How was that going to change as God took up the cause of the people of Judah? (1:4-6, 9-10)

How complete would the fall of Nineveh be? (1:12-15)

Read Nahum 2:1-13.
But after being so specific in his prophecy, Nahum became somewhat sarcastic as he warned Nineveh to prepare for "an attacker." What were the Ninevites supposed to do? (2:1)

We know that the Babylonians and Medes had formed an alliance and attacked Assyria. What images were given for those attackers of Nineveh? (2:3-4)

What images were given for the people in Nineveh? (2:5-10)

Nahum compared Nineveh to a lions' den, where once the lions had roamed and killed and had their own way. But Nahum's question is, "Where now is the lions' den?" All the pride and power of Nineveh would be suddenly destroyed. What simple statement explains how such a vast power could fall so quickly? (2:13)

Read Nahum 3:1-19.
In what ways would Nineveh be humiliated? (3:1-7)

What other unique image was given to describe the fall of Nineveh into the hands of its enemies? (3:12)

What hope was left for Nineveh? (3:13, 17-19)

What's Your Verdict?

Archaeologists confirm Nahum's prophecy. Nineveh, as great a city as it was, never was rebuilt. The tragedy is not so much in Nineveh's final fall—it seems an appropriate end for such a brutal and savage city. The bigger tragedy is that God had previously spared the city, but the people had taken His forgiveness lightly and immediately returned to their wicked ways.

Habakkuk

As we move from Nahum to the next prophet, the focus shifts from God's judgment on the wicked to His chastisement of His own people. The next writer is Habakkuk, and his book breaks out of the traditional prophetic writing style that you've seen so far. Habakkuk doesn't bring a message directly from God to the people. Instead, he recorded a dialogue between himself and God. Habakkuk asked some hard questions of God, but he also received some good answers. His dialog took place at the crucial time in Judah's history just before the Babylonians defeated Jerusalem and carried the people off into captivity. It is likely that Habakkuk lived to see his prophecy come true.

Read Habakkuk 1:1-17.
What was Habakkuk's basic complaint to God? (Habakkuk 1:1-4)

No doubt that after Habakkuk's accusation, he expected God to explain what was going on. And God did, but it wasn't the answer Habakkuk expected. In effect, Habakkuk had asked, "Why aren't You doing something about all this injustice?" And God immediately replied that He *was* doing something. What was God doing? (1:5-6)

Getting Personal — *What injustices would you like for God to act on today?*

How did God describe these people whom He was going to use to accomplish His plans? Be specific (1:7-11).

God's reply really confused Habakkuk. The prophet would probably have been happier to hear that God wasn't going to do anything at all than to discover exactly what His plans were. What was Habakkuk's second complaint? (1:12-17)

Read Habakkuk 2:1-20.
What action did Habakkuk determine to take until he received an answer from God? (2:1)

God knew that a lot of people probably had the same questions as Habakkuk. So what did He tell Habakkuk to do? (2:2-3)

In retrospect, it's simple to see that God knew exactly what was going to happen. (But in the "present tense" it's not always so simple to believe that God knows what's best for us.) Yes, He was definitely going to allow His people to be overpowered and taken away. But after 70 years He would just as surely allow them to return to their homeland. Habakkuk, who wasn't aware of the whole picture, could only see that God was about to chastise His sinful people by using other people who were even more sinful.

God knew exactly what kind of people the Babylonians were. He gave a graphic description of the Babylonians as if they were a single person. What are some of the specific charges God had against Babylon? (2:4-19)

But scattered throughout the description of the Babylonians, God sprinkled some promises to Habakkuk. What assurances did God provide His prophet? (2:4, 14, 20)

Read Habakkuk 3:1-19.
Habakkuk asked no more piercing questions at this point. Perhaps he no longer felt the need to know why God decides to allow certain things. It seems that he came to the realization that it was more important to remember *who* was in control than to know *why* He operated the way He did. And Habakkuk ended his book with a powerful and positive affirmation of

What's Your Verdict?

praise to God. What simple thing did Habakkuk request at this point? (3:2)

Habakkuk was reminded of many of the things God had done for the Israelites in the past (3:3-15). Perhaps he was able to see and hear portions of the events he described (based on his phrases such as "God came" in verse 3 and "I saw" in verse 7). And as he recalled instances like God's ability to induce plagues at will (v. 5), part the waters of the sea (v. 8), and make the sun and moon stand still (v. 11), Habakkuk realized that God had never had any problem delivering His people from hostile nations. Most of the third chapter of Habakkuk is a type of hymn (complete with a few musical notations) to help listeners remember God's goodness throughout the years and build their trust in Him.

After being reminded of God's previous dealings with His people, how did Habakkuk feel? (3:16)

Getting Personal — *When you think about God's previous dealings with you, how does it make you feel?*

Having determined to "wait patiently" for the Babylonians to attack (3:16), you might think Habakkuk would feel depressed. But he wasn't. Reread Habakkuk 3:17-19 and describe his state of mind as he ended his writings.

Zephaniah
Read Zephaniah 1:1-18.
The last prophet we meet in this session is Zephaniah. One of his main distinctions is that he was descended from royalty—specifically, King Hezekiah of Judah. Perhaps Zephaniah was of a higher social level than some of the other prophets. Do you think his status affected his message? (Zephaniah 1:1-3)

Watchmen Who Wouldn't Quit

Zephaniah prophesied during the reign of King Josiah. During this time, Judah was doing pretty well from a political/military standpoint. Spiritually, the people would experience some degree of revival under King Josiah, but would soon return to their path of spiritual decay. And Zephaniah's message was that Judah should be aware of the coming "Day of the Lord."

For what specific sins was Judah going to be judged? (1:4-6)

What was the attitude of the people of Judah? (1:12-13)

What kind of judgment was Judah to expect? (1:14-18)

Read Zephaniah 2:1-15.
Do you think God would have canceled His judgment on Judah if the people had listened to Zephaniah (and the other prophets) and repented? (2:1-3)

Read Zephaniah 3:1-20.
Zephaniah didn't just single out Judah for God's judgment. He also predicted judgment on the land of the Philistines, Moab, Ammon, Cush, and Assyria—Nineveh in particular (Chapter 2). But in Chapter 3, Zephaniah specifically addressed the future of Jerusalem. When compared to the heathen nations, Jerusalem didn't come out looking much better than any of those ungodly places. What spiritual weaknesses were evident in Jerusalem? (3:1-4)

Getting Personal — *Are any of these spiritual weaknesses evident in your own life? If so, which ones?*

How does Zephaniah describe God in contrast to sinful Jerusalem? (3:5)

What's Your Verdict?

Like so many of the prophets you've already seen, Zephaniah followed his description of God's coming judgment with the scene the people could look forward to *after* God's judgment. What would be different about the people once they had gone through God's judgment? (3:11-13)

What specific promises did God leave the people of Judah through the words of Zephaniah? (3:14-20)

JOURNEY INWARD

Although every session in this book has touched on the issue, perhaps we need to stop and specifically address the topic of **God's judgment.** No matter whether you or anyone else feels that it's fair for God to pass judgment on anyone, it's a biblical fact that He does. But it's also a fact that no other judge is more fair in judgment than God is. And you should always remember that the Lord "is patient with you, not wanting anyone to perish, but everyone to come to repentance" (2 Peter 3:9).

A lot of theological problems could be avoided if people spent the same amount of time in repentance that they spend accusing God of unfairness. No one claims to be able to understand completely the complexity of God, yet we all occasionally go through periods where we seem to think we have a more complete grasp of the facts and can make better decisions than God. When that happens, God will usually deal with us gently and set us straight. But if we develop a defiant attitude and continually try to outguess God and live in disobedience, He is forced to discipline us. And again, we need to remember that "the Lord disciplines those He loves" (Hebrews 12:6).

It's not as if God is just waiting for you to make one little mistake so He can exile you to a foreign country. But it is true that because He loves you, He will try to set you on the right path if you mistakenly or intentionally fall into a sin.

So what can the minor prophets teach us? First, Nahum makes it clear that God doesn't take sin lightly. After sending God's word through Jonah, one of the greatest cities in the world had "repented." But Nineveh's repentance was not lasting, and they quickly fell back into their old, sinful habits. What sins in your own life do you seem to keep asking God's forgiveness for? And what do you think it would take to motivate you to put those sins behind you once and for all?

Habakkuk showed us that God will help us work out even our hardest questions and problems if we keep at it and trust Him to come through for us. What questions are you struggling with concerning God and His relationship to the world? And what problems do you have that may seem unsolvable for you?

From Zephaniah we get the assurance that God will come to set things straight—possibly sooner than we might expect. When that time comes, it will be too late for those who have opposed Him all along. And it may even be an uncomfortable time for His own people who haven't been living up to His standards. What things would you change in your life if you knew Jesus were returning to earth first thing tomorrow morning? And who all should you be praying for and talking to in order for them to avoid the judgment of God?

It's a tragic mistake to take the judgment of God lightly. Just as it came to the people of Israel and Judah, the prophets make it clear that it will again take place. But Christians need not fear it if they live in awareness that it is coming. When the judgment of God takes place again, those who have been faithful will receive rewards, not condemnation (Romans 8:1; Ephesians 6:8).

Habakkuk had a positive attitude that we all should try to imitate. He saw the world falling apart around him and could find no justice in what was happening, but he was still able to express his confidence in God. To close

What's Your Verdict?

this session, reread Habakkuk 3:17-19 and paraphrase it to include your own apparently unsolvable problems that you have just recorded. ("Though I have no money and my spouse is too hard on me, though my children are delinquents and my boss won't give me a raise, etc., etc., etc., yet I will rejoice in the Lord.") Write your paraphrase below.

And don't just *say* you will rejoice in the Lord. Really do it. It's not easy to do, but it's not nearly as difficult as standing before God on Judgment Day and trying to explain just why you weren't willing to give up those "little" sins. The prophets gave this matter a lot of thought. You should too. So what's your verdict?

KEY VERSE

"The Lord your God is with you, He is mighty to save. He will take great delight in you, He will quiet you with His love, He will rejoice over you with singing" (Zephaniah 3:17).

Joe and Charlie were facing another boring weekend until Tracey and Beth came along.

12

WHAT DO YOU EXPECT?
(Haggai, Zechariah, Malachi)

[Joe and Charlie are walking out of work and having their usual Friday afternoon discussion.]

Joe:	So, do you want to do something this weekend?
Charlie:	Sure. What do you want to do?
Joe:	I don't know. What do you want to do?
Charlie:	I don't know. We could play some ball.
Joe:	Nah. Too many of the guys will be doing stuff. We'd never get up a game.
Charlie:	The late-night TV movie tomorrow is going to be *Godzilla vs. The Expandable Mole People*. I love to see Godzilla poach those little guys with his fire breath.
Joe:	But we've already seen it nine times. We could lip sync the lines by now, except the actors are speaking in Japanese. Maybe we could take a drive into the city.
Charlie:	There's nothing happening and nowhere to go. Hey! Why don't we grab some dinner and go to the free concert in the park?
Joe:	No way! Those concerts are always so boring. The music is dull.
Charlie:	So what do you want to do?
Joe:	I don't know. What do you want to do?

[Enter Tracey and Beth.]

Tracey:	Hi, guys! Whatcha' doing?
Charlie:	We're, uh, making big plans for the weekend.

Watchmen Who Wouldn't Quit

Beth:	Oh, shoot. That's too bad.
Joe:	Why is that bad?
Tracey:	We were going to . . . oh, never mind.
Charlie:	No, no. Go ahead and tell us what you were going to say.
Tracey:	Oh, we were going to ask you guys out for tomorrow night.
Beth:	We were going to cook you some dinner and then suggest we go to the free concert in the park. But since you guys have big plans . . .
Charlie:	I, uh, don't think it's too late to change our plans.
Joe:	Yeah. We're busy, sure, but we're flexible. Besides, I really love those concerts in the park—the atmosphere and music and all.
Tracey:	Great! See you at, say, 6:30 tomorrow night?
Charlie:	We'll be there.

[Tracey and Beth exit.]

Joe:	Wow! I can't believe they would ask us to do something with them.
Charlie:	Yeah. I've got to get busy. I'll need some gas money . . .
Joe:	I've got to have some new shoes . . .
Charlie:	Maybe we should take them some flowers . . .
Joe:	Sure. Something simple, not too fancy. And you could stand a haircut.
Charlie:	Well, let me clue you. When you get those new shoes, you'd better grab some Odor-Eaters too.
Joe:	OK. OK.
Charlie:	Let's go!

. . . .

Isn't it amazing how life can change drastically when there is something special to look forward to? Joe and Charlie were facing "just another boring weekend" that held no expectation of joy or excitement. But all it took to change their attitudes was a special event. (Even a casual dinner and free concert become special when they are shared with the right people.)

Maybe you can relate to the feeling. Perhaps your attitude toward life changes just before your birthday, Christmas, the end of a big project, or other significant event. If you have nothing to look forward to, life can get kind of dull if you don't watch out.

What Do You Expect?

JOURNEY ONWARD

The three minor prophets that you will meet in this session knew what it was like to live in expectation of big events. Most of the prophets you've already seen were anticipating the gloom that would accompany the fall of Jerusalem and captivity of the people. But the three in this session lived during or after the exile, so their focus was on a time when the Messiah would come and establish a kingdom the way it *should* be.

Read Haggai 1:1-15.
The first of this session's minor prophets was a man named Haggai. His prophecies took place during four months of the reign of King Darius (the Persian king who sent Daniel to the lions' den). During this time, a number of the Jews had been granted permission to return to Jerusalem and begin rebuilding their temple that the Babylonians had destroyed. They had returned to Jerusalem, sure enough, but what was the problem? (Haggai 1:1-4)

If you remember what you read in Ezra and Nehemiah (in Book 3, *Tunes, Tales, & Truths*), you know that the Israelites had faced some opposition from the people living in the area of Jerusalem when they tried to rebuild the temple. But God saw that the root problem was laziness. So Haggai was sent to the people with a message. In what ways was their inactivity having an effect on their lives? (1:5-11)

Before their captivity, the people had been reluctant to listen to what God had to say to them. How had their attitude changed during the 70 years of their exile? (1:12-15)

Getting Personal – *Are you ever reluctant to listen to what God has to say to you? Why or why not?*

Watchmen Who Wouldn't Quit

Read Haggai 2:1-23.
How did the new temple compare to the one Solomon had built? (2:1-3)

What promise did God make to the people? (2:6-9)

Then God (through Haggai) left the priests something to think about. Reread Haggai 2:11-14 and notice the two questions God asked them. God wanted the priests to realize that when a ceremonially "clean" object came into contact with an unclean object, in most cases the unclean object would defile the clean object. The people were unclean in the sense that they had been ignoring God's instructions to rebuild the temple. Because of their disobedience, their offerings were considered defiled. And because they had been disregarding God's will, God had not blessed their harvests. But after they rebuilt the temple, what was going to be different? (2:15-19)

What special distinction did God give Zerubbabel, the man who headed up the project to rebuild the temple? (2:20-23)

Zechariah

Another special person (besides Haggai) under the leadership of Zerubbabel was the Prophet Zechariah, who had returned to the Jerusalem area with the other Babylonian exiles. Zechariah was a priest, and he didn't hesitate to pass on the words and visions that God gave him. He started his writings by describing how God's anger had been directed against the forefathers of the people, but that when the people realized that they should obey God instead of opposing Him, they repented.

Skim Zechariah 1:1–8:23.

Zechariah then described eight visions he saw. He also recorded the explanations that were provided him for each of the visions (though not all of them have clear and specific meanings). Read each of Zechariah's descriptions of his visions and match each one to the interpretation you think is closest to the true meaning.

What Do You Expect?

MATCH THE VISION

Vision	Interpretation
A man among myrtle trees with horses behind him (1:7-17)	God would send His servant, "the Branch" (Jesus), to remove the sin of the people.
Four horns and four craftsmen (1:18-21)	A curse was being sent out to the thieves and lawbreakers in the land.
A man with a measuring line (2:1-13)	God's messengers would go in all directions to deal with the nations of the earth.
New clothes for the high priest (3:1-10)	The temple would be rebuilt and the people would again prosper.
A lampstand and olive trees (4:1-14)	Jerusalem would again be populated and the nations who had persecuted "the apple of God's eye" would suffer.
A flying scroll (5:1-4)	Zerubbabel would complete the temple which would be attended to by two people. (These two would be symbolic of Jesus, who would serve as both King [the golden lampstand] and Priest [the olive oil].)
A woman in a basket (5:5-11)	Judah's enemies would be terrified and defeated.
Four chariots between two mountains (6:1-8)	Israel's wickedness would be removed from the land of Judah, though allowed to flourish in the land of Babylon.

Watchmen Who Wouldn't Quit

Zechariah saw all of these visions during the same night, so it's not too surprising that they aren't described in great detail. (How would you like to have eight consecutive visions and then be responsible to recall and write them all down for future generations?) Besides, the visions were a preview leading up to what God really wanted Zechariah to do. What were God's instructions to Zechariah? (6:9-13)

It was unusual for a priest to be crowned like a king, but this was a symbolic gesture. God was trying to prepare His people for the coming of a ruler who would serve both as a king and a priest (repeating the significance of Zechariah's fifth vision).

Read Zechariah 9:1-17.
Zechariah had a lot to say about the coming of "The Branch"—God's Messiah who was to rule the earth someday. We've already seen that He was to be both King and Priest (6:13) and would fulfill those roles by rebuilding the temple of God (6:12-13). As King, how would He come to His people? (9:9)

What kind of rule would this King have? (9:10)

Skim Zechariah 10:1–14:21.
But this King would fall out of favor with the people. At one point, God asked Zechariah to role play the part of a "Good Shepherd" who was sent to replace a number of selfish, greedy shepherds in overseeing a "flock marked for slaughter" (11:4-7). How did the flock respond to their new Good Shepherd? (11:8)

How much did they value the work of their Good Shepherd? (11:12)

What Do You Expect?

This amount of money was about what someone would expect to pay for a slave, so you can see that the Good Shepherd wasn't very highly valued. What happened to the money that they felt He was worth? (11:13)

What was to happen to this Shepherd? (13:7-8)

How would the people feel about their Good Shepherd after He had left them? (12:10)

What would happen after the Good Shepherd was rejected? (11:16-17)

Zechariah saw that things were going to get pretty bad on the earth after the Messiah was rejected. Some of his prophecies seem to refer to the Romans, who were in power when Jesus was born, and who eventually destroyed the Jewish temple (in A.D. 70). Other of Zechariah's predictions were in reference to the end times and the Antichrist. But like the other prophets, Zechariah saw beyond all the bad stuff and assured those who would listen that God (and His people) would ultimately come out victorious. Describe the scene that will precede the coming of the Lord (14:1-2).

What major events did Zechariah prophesy would occur when God comes to reign? (14:3-9)

What is in store for those who refuse to turn to God? (14:12-15)

What kinds of worship habits will take place during this time? (14:16-21)

Malachi

And now, at last, we finally reach the prophet you've been waiting for (since he's the last one)—Malachi. He is not only the last in the order of the books of the Old Testament, but also very likely the last prophet chronologically. His focus was on the spiritual apathy that God's people experienced after returning from Exile and rebuilding the temple.

Read Malachi 1:1-14.
Malachi began by reaffirming the love God had for the Israelites (Malachi 1:1-5). But immediately afterward, he presented a number of hard questions (along with answers that the people didn't want to hear). First God wanted to know why, since He was their ruler, the people weren't showing Him respect. The people asked *how* they had shown disrespect. How did God answer them, and what did He want them to do about it? (Malachi 1:6-14)

Read Malachi 2:1-17.
Then God had a command for the priests to shape up or suffer the consequences (2:1-2). How had the performance of the priests changed since the time of Levi, the person from whom all the priests were descended? (2:3-9)

[NOTE: *Offal* (NIV) refers to the insides of an animal that were taken outside the camp and burned when the animal was sacrificed to God.]

Malachi then reminded the people how Judah had been unfaithful to God by "marrying the daughter of a foreign god" (2:11). What else had the people done to grieve God? (2:17)

What Do You Expect?

Getting Personal – *Have you done anything recently to grieve God? If so, what?*

Read Malachi 3:1-18.
The people had also "robbed" God. How? (3:6-9)

It's not that God was reluctant to share anything or everything He had with His people. But He wanted to give it to them rather than have them withhold their offerings. What challenge did God present to the people? (3:10-12)

What other accusation did God bring against the people, and what did some of them do to correct the problem? (3:13-18)

Read Malachi 4:1-6.
Like many of the prophets before him, Malachi reported what God told him about the last days. What is in store for the wicked people? (4:1)

What does the future hold for those who remain true to God? (4:2-3)

But the best news that Malachi brought was that before God sent His final judgment on the world, He first would send His messenger to prepare the way (3:1). This messenger is referred to as "Elijah," which means that the person would have the same characteristics as the Old Testament prophet, Elijah. What was this messenger to do? (4:5-6)

Watchmen Who Wouldn't Quit

And if you're the kind of person who likes to peek ahead to see how the story comes out, you can discover in Matthew 11:11-15 who this Elijah person turned out to be.

It's interesting to note the last word in the Old Testament—*curse*. From the first session in this **BibleLog** Series until this one, you have seen Old Testament characters having to decide whether they would choose to obey God or follow their own whims. And the Old Testament ends with the same basic options. Some people refused to believe the prophets and became skeptical that God would ever rectify the injustices they saw in the world. Without God to depend on, they had no sense of expectation and could never live fulfilled lives. Others, however, were looking to the future with great expectation. They heard and believed that God would send a Person who would provide peace, redemption, mercy, and forgiveness. And their belief was not in vain.

JOURNEY INWARD

Let's focus on developing the benefits of **expectation**. The opening of this session pointed out that it doesn't always take a lot to boost our outlook of the future. But if we keep our ears open to what the prophets have been saying, we should be so filled with expectation that we need lead shoes to stay down to earth.

It's important to bear in mind that the prophets were right on the nose in their prophecies concerning the first coming of Jesus—His birthplace, suffering, death, and so forth. And those same prophets spoke of a second coming that hasn't yet occurred. We have absolutely no reason to doubt that those prophecies are any less accurate. So the question is: What difference do those prophecies make in your day-to-day life?

If you're like most people, you've probably had your share of doubt, failure, depression, embarrassment, humiliation, pain, bad judgment, mistakes, confusion, and who-knows-what else. These things hit everybody from time to time. And if you have no sense of expectation that God will be there to see you through them, they can stay with you a long, long time. But if you *have* developed a sense of expectation for God to be there for you and see you through whatever is getting you down, your problems are likely to disappear much more quickly.

What Do You Expect?

On the following chart, imagine yourself in each of the situations. Then think through the potential results—first, as if you had no expectation of God to carry you through the situation; and second, with the assurance that you could count on God to take you through the problem and eventually give you peace.

SITUATION	NOT EXPECTING GOD'S HELP	EXPECTING GOD'S HELP
A close friend or family member dies.		
A friend tells you he/she is thinking about suicide.		
You lose your job.		
You have an accident that leaves you unable to walk.		
You've been fighting with your spouse a lot, and you unexpectedly inherit $100,000 from a distant relative.		
Nothing specific is wrong, but you just can't get over strong feelings of depression.		

The last two situations may have caused you to shift your thinking a little. Sometimes we prepare ourselves to expect God to help when things get really terrible. And He will be there during those times. But we must be careful to expect God's guidance during good times and "average" times as well.

God can and will make a difference in your life. And as you learn to count on His help more and more, and grow to expect Him to be there for you, there's nothing you won't be able to face. As we leave the Old Testament behind with the eager anticipation that God will fulfill all the promises He made to the prophets, we should also try to leave behind our old ways of thinking. Let's look to the future instead with the confident expectation that God is going ahead of us through any troublesome situations we might face.

KEY VERSE
" 'Not by might nor by power, but by My Spirit,' says the Lord Almighty" (Zechariah 4:6).

BEFORE YOU LEAVE

Wait. Wait. Wait. Wait. Wait. Don't feel like you're finished with Bible study just because you got to the end of the Old Testament in this session. The **BibleLog** Series was designed to give you the big picture of the Old Testament, but there are thousands and thousands of little pictures for you to go back through and become more familiar with. Try to spend a little time every day, because God will usually help you discover something you missed before, and certain passages that didn't seem to hit the target the first time might be just what you need next time.

But if you want a little break, we'd appreciate it if you'd fill out the form on page 179 and send it back to us. Be honest in your evaluation, because we want to develop products that you like to use. Thanks a lot.

If you haven't yet completed **BibleLog Thru the Old Testament** Series, all 4 books are available at your local Christian bookstore. And if you're looking for a challenge in the New Testament, look for the **BibleLog Thru the New Testament** Series.

CERTIFICATE
Congratulations,

_____
(name)

Now you have the big picture of the Old Testament. You have successfully completed the four books of the **BibleLog Thru the Old Testament** Series, surveying primary themes, characters, and key verses of Scripture. You are to be commended for steadfastness, enthusiasm, and perseverance. May God richly bless you as you continue to learn more about Him.

GETTING TOGETHER

A Leader's Guide for Small Groups

Before you jump into this leader's guide in all the excitement of preparing for Session 1, take time to read these introductory pages.

Because the basic Bible content of the study is covered inductively in 12 chapters, group members should work through each assigned chapter before attending the small group meeting. This isn't always easy for busy adults, so encourage group members with a phone call or note between some of the meetings. Help them manage their time by pointing out how they can cover a few pages in a few minutes daily, and having them identify a regular time that they can devote to the **BibleLog** study.

Notice that each session is structured to include the following:

- Session Topic—a brief statement of purpose for the session.
- Icebreaker—an activity to help group members get better acquainted with the session topic and/or each other.
- Discussion Questions—a list of questions to encourage group participation.
- Optional Activities—supplemental ideas that will enhance your study.
- Assignment—directions for preparation and suggestions for memorization of key Scriptures.

Here are a few tips that can lead to more effective small group studies:

- Pray for each group member, asking the Lord to help you create an atmosphere where everyone will feel free to share with each other and you.
- Encourage group members to bring their Bibles to each session. This series is based on the *New International Version*, but it is good to have several translations on hand for purposes of comparison.
- Start on time. This is especially important for the first meeting because it will set the pattern for the rest of the course.

- ❑ Begin with prayer, asking the Holy Spirit to open hearts and minds and to give understanding so that truth will be applied.
- ❑ Involve everyone. As learners, we retain only 10 percent of what we hear, 20 percent of what we see, 65 percent of what we hear and see, *but* 90 percent of what we hear, see, and do.
- ❑ Promote a relaxed environment. Arrange your chairs in a circle or semi-circle. This promotes eye contact among members and encourages more dynamic discussion. Be relaxed in your own attitude and manner.

1

Session Topic: God is the source of our confidence.

Icebreaker
Distribute pens and note cards. Have group members describe an area of their lives where they need more confidence. Collect the papers and read each one aloud. Ask the group to guess which member "belongs" with the description.

Discussion Questions
1. How does your conversion experience compare to Isaiah's experience?
2. Brainstorm ways you can stand firm in your faith.
3. What was Isaiah's confidence based on?
4. How did Isaiah become conscious of his own position and the power of God?

Prayer
Suggest that each person ask God for confidence to overcome the weak areas of his or her life.

Optional Activities
1. Share a brief overview of Israel's physical and spiritual conditions during the time of the prophets.
2. Examine the characteristics of a true prophet as described in Deuteronomy 13:1-5; 18:9-22; Amos 3:7. Have the group write a profile of a prophet.

Assignment
1. Complete Session 2.
2. Memorize Isaiah 7:9.

2

Session Topic: Hope is the certainty that God is there to help us when we need support.

Icebreakers (*choose one*)
1. Distribute various sections of newspapers and have the group make a list of situations in world affairs, business, sports, and local news that seem hopeless. Ask: **How do you think Isaiah would respond if he read these newspapers?**
2. Ask: **How are you able to stay hopeful, looking at the depressing things going on in the world around you?**

Discussion Questions
1. Where did Isaiah place his confidence?
2. In what or whom have you placed your confidence?
3. How was Isaiah able to sustain such a high level of hope?
4. What are some reasons that you should have hope regarding specific problems in your life?

Prayer
Ask God to give each person the ability to look beyond his or her problems to possible solutions.

Optional Activities
Divide into pairs to study and report on Isaiah's prophecies that are fulfilled in the New Testament: 7:14 (Matthew 1:22-23); 9:1-2 (Matthew 4:12-16); 9:6 (Luke 2:11); 11:1 (Luke 3:23, 32); 11:2 (Luke 3:22); 40:3-6 (Matthew 3:1-3); 42:1-4 (Matthew 12:15-21); 42:6 (Luke 2:29-32); 50:6 (Matthew 26:67); 53:3 (Luke 23:18); 53:7 (Matthew 27:12-14); 53:9 (Matthew 27:57-60); 53:12 (Mark 15:28); 61:1-2 (Luke 4:17-21). Sing hymns such as: "Day Is Dying in the West" (based on Isaiah 6:3) and "He Was Wounded for Our Transgressions" (based on Isaiah 53).

Assignment
1. Complete Session 3.
2. Memorize Isaiah 40:31.

3

Session Topic: When we face loneliness, despair, and rejection, our major source of companionship can be God.

Icebreakers *(choose one)*
1. As the group arrives, play a few recordings of songs about loneliness and rejection. Have the group compare the songs of loneliness they listed on page 37.
2. Recall a time when you felt lonely or rejected. Share how you responded to that loneliness.

Discussion Questions
1. How did Jeremiah describe the spiritual condition of Judah?
2. Should a Christian ever feel lonely? Why or why not?
3. What was Jeremiah's strategy for loneliness?
4. How can you apply Jeremiah's strategy in dealing with despair and rejection?

Prayer
Ask God to help each person develop a sense of His presence whenever he or she faces loneliness.

Optional Activities
1. Divide into teams to study Jeremiah's messages during Josiah's reign. Make the following assignments: Team 1 (2:1–3:5); Team 2 (3:6–6:30); Team 3 (7:1–10:25); Team 4 (18:1–20:18).
2. Do a word study of the name *Jeremiah*. Point out that Jeremiah literally means "Yahweh throws," suggesting that God lays a foundation.

Assignment
1. Complete Session 4.
2. Memorize Jeremiah 17:7-8.

4

Session Topic: God wants us to draw near and share our burdens with Him when we face crises.

Icebreaker
Distribute note cards and have group members write on their cards crises or difficulties they are experiencing. Collect the cards and redistribute them to the group. Take a few minutes to silently pray for the person on your card who is experiencing a crisis.

Discussion Questions
1. Picture yourself in Babylon, with your country and church destroyed. How would you have reacted to the suffering associated with the Exile?
2. What are some typical responses to different types of crises?
3. How do *you* respond to crisis?

Prayer
Ask God to help each group member to pray for the person on his or her note card during the next week.

Optional Activities
1. Obtain a copy of the spiritual "There Is a Balm in Gilead." Read Jeremiah 8:22 and compare the Scripture with the song lyrics.
2. Ask volunteers to set up a crisis prayer chain for the group.
3. Invite a crisis counselor from your church or community to speak to your group. Encourage the speaker to share a few case studies as well as typical reactions to different types of crises.

Assignment
1. Complete Session 5.
2. Memorize Jeremiah 33:3.

5

Session Topic: Rather than turning to occult practices, we should seek truth and wisdom from God for our futures.

Icebreaker
Distribute a few tabloids and newspapers at this session. Have group members read a few articles that focus on various supernatural or occult practices. Ask: **Why are people so fascinated with the supernatural?**

Discussion Questions
1. Why are people more apt to believe that supernatural truth can be found in horoscopes, Tarot cards, and channeling rather than in the Bible?
2. How do you know that God isn't the only supernatural force in the world?
3. Do you find it difficult to accept God's omnipresence, omniscience, and omnipotence? Why or why not?
4. How would your curiosity about the future change if you truly began to think of God as omnipresent, omniscient, and omnipotent?

Prayer
Ask God to help each group member sense His presence, wisdom, and power daily.

Optional Activities
1. Skim Ezekiel 1–18 to identify the prophet's message. Explain that Ezekiel placed special emphasis on the glory of God.
2. Work in pairs to examine Ezekiel's message about the siege of Jerusalem in chapters 4–5. Each pair should list the symbolic acts of Ezekiel. Ask: **How would you have reacted to Ezekiel's actions?**

Assignment
1. Complete Session 6.
2. Memorize Ezekiel 14:6.

6

Session Topic: We need to be more accountable to God and the people around us.

Icebreaker
Ask group members to share the last time they acted irresponsibly toward God, their families, friends, bosses, or church. Pair up and compare your responses for similarities and differences.

Discussion Questions
1. Brainstorm some ways that you can act more responsibly toward your family, friends, boss, church, and God.
2. How can you sacrifice your own desires in order to be more responsible to others?
3. What literary devices can be found in the Book of Ezekiel?
4. How can you act more responsibly during the next week?

Prayer
Ask God to give each group member a new heart and spirit.

Optional Activities
1. Study the literary devices used by Ezekiel: proverbs (12:22-23; 16:44; 18:2-3); visions (1–3; 8–11; 37; 40–48); parables (17; 24:1-14); symbolic acts (4–5; 12; 24:15-27); allegories (16–17).
2. Sing or play a recording of the hymn, "Gracious Spirit, Dwell with Me," which is based on Ezekiel 36:26.
3. Have group members choose partners and share one way he or she plans to act more accountable during the next week. Explain that each person will hold his or her partner accountable for the decision he or she makes.

Assignment
1. Complete Session 7.
2. Memorize Ezekiel 36:26.

7

Session Topic: God wants us to take a courageous stand against negative peer pressure.

Icebreakers *(choose one)*
1. Imagine you're flying to England for a vacation. Suddenly your jet is hijacked. You're ushered off the plane to a dormitory filled with people from all over the world who only speak their native tongues. You try to find out what is going on, but you can't understand anyone. Dinnertime comes and you discover that the main dietary source is cold potato soup (which you hate). Next, you learn that your name has been changed and you will spend days studying foreign literature. How would you respond?
2. Compare the captivities of American hostages in Iran, Lebanon, and Vietnam with Daniel's hostage situation in Babylon.

Discussion Questions
1. What was the Babylonian influence on Daniel?
2. Would you be able to trust in God, defy your country's laws, and be willing to give up your life rather than serve or worship someone or something other than God?
3. Describe the worst peer pressure you face.

Prayer
Ask God to help each group member remember to consider alternative responses to the negative peer pressures they face.

Optional Activities
1. Do word studies of the names *Daniel* and *Belteshazzar*. Explain that *Daniel* means "God is (my) judge." Point out that *Belteshazzar* means "Bel protect his life."
2. Research the possibilities of forming a support group. Point out that positive support can help group members overcome negative pressures.

Assignment
1. Complete Session 8.
2. Memorize Daniel 3:28.

8

Session Topic: God can do great things for people who are not ego-centered.

Icebreakers (*choose one*)
1. Ask: **What is the difference between valid self-worth and false pride? Share some examples of each.**
2. Read Daniel 6:26-27. Ask each group member to share how God rescued and saved him or her from eternal destruction. If unsaved group members are present, offer them the opportunity to accept Christ as their personal Savior.

Discussion Questions
1. What talents or accomplishments do you have that you are proud of?
2. Is there a possibility that you may be a little too proud of one or more of your talents or abilities?
3. Identify some areas of false pride in your life.
4. How can you deal with areas of false pride?

Prayer
Ask God to help group members deal with areas of false pride and develop lives that aren't ego-centered.

Optional Activities
1. Ask several group members to write a short skit about Daniel and the lions' den. Suggest that the skit be based on a lion's point of view. Have the group members perform their skit for the rest of the group.
2. Ask group members to draw their perceptions of the four beasts of Daniel's vision as described in chapter 7. Compare the drawings and discuss the significance and possible interpretations of each beast.

Assignment
1. Complete Session 9.
2. Memorize Daniel 6:26-27.

9

Session Topic: God wants us to honor our commitment to being faithful to Him in many areas of our lives.

Icebreakers (*choose one*)
1. Distribute note cards and ask each group member to write a definition of *faithfulness*. Collect the cards and read each definition aloud. Then develop a complete definition and display it on a poster or chalkboard.
2. Share the names of people you know who exhibit the quality of faithfulness.

Discussion Questions
1. Do others consider you a faithful person? Why or why not?
2. In what areas of your life have you been unfaithful to God?
3. How can you obtain the blessings mentioned in Joel?
4. What are some ways you can be faithful to God in the following categories—Social, Mental, Physical, Spiritual?

Prayer
Ask each group member to complete the following sentence prayer: **Lord, help me to be more faithful in** (social, mental, physical, or spiritual) **areas of my life.**

Optional Activities
1. Plan to do word studies on the names *Hosea, Joshua,* and *Jesus*. Explain that the names are all derived from the same Hebrew root word meaning "salvation."
2. Have several group members research and report on the themes of the Books of Hosea, Joel, and Amos.

Assignment
1. Complete Session 10.
2. Memorize Joel 2:13.

10

Session Topic: Security without dependence on God is false security.

Icebreakers *(choose one)*
1. List all the "security blankets" that you have used in the past month, such as locks, money, car, etc.
2. Share the name of one person or thing that you have depended on to give you a sense of security. Then describe and compare feelings of security and insecurity.

Discussion Questions
1. What are some of the sources of insecurity?
2. Are you dependent on God for security, or do you rely more on your own skills and abilities?
3. Are any of your "security blankets" preventing you from building a trusting relationship with God? Why or why not?
4. Review Micah 7:18-19 and list five things Micah affirmed about God in these verses.

Prayer
Pray that each person will begin putting his or her security in God's hands by consciously seeking His guidance and care for his or her life.

Optional Activities
1. Ask several group members to research and report on the themes of Obadiah, Jonah, and Micah.
2. Read Matthew 12:39-41. Explain that Jonah is the only prophet to whom Jesus likened Himself. Discuss how Jonah's experience is similar to Christ's death, burial, and resurrection.

Assignment
1. Complete Session 11.
2. Memorize Micah 7:18-19.

11

Session Topic: Christians need not fear the judgment of God as long as they live in the awareness that it is coming.

Icebreaker
Ask: **If you knew Jesus was returning to earth first thing tomorrow morning, how would you feel? What things would you want to change about your life? Would you have friends or family that you would want to talk to in order to help them avoid the judgment of God?**

Discussion Questions
1. Skim the Book of Nahum and list any attributes of God that you find. Determine which attributes characterize God's grace and which characterize His justice.
2. Is it possible to separate the truth of God's grace from the reality of His justice? Why or why not?
3. Review Habakkuk 3 and identify the three qualities in Habakkuk's prayer.
4. Who is one person with whom you need to discuss the tragedy of taking the judgment of God lightly?

Prayer
Pray that each person will share the message of God's justice and grace with someone who needs to know how to avoid the judgment of God.

Optional Activities
1. Ask several group members to research and report on the themes of Nahum, Habakkuk, and Zephaniah.
2. Ask a judge in your church or community to share his ideas on justice with your group.

Assignment
1. Complete Session 12.
2. Memorize Zephaniah 3:17.

12

Session Topic: Fulfillment of our expectations comes only as we draw near to God and respond to His Word.

Icebreaker
Write down where you expect to be 10 years from now in each of the following categories: personal finance, business/occupation, marital status, spirituality, health/beauty. Then share how you responded with the rest of the group.

Discussion Questions
1. How can we realize our expectations?
2. What prevented the Jews of Malachi's day from receiving God's blessings?
3. Identify some of the harmful attitudes and actions revealed in the Book of Malachi.
4. Brainstorm some ways that you can transform harmful attitudes and actions into positive, healthy patterns.

Prayer
Spend some time in silent meditation. Encourage group members to thank God for His great blessings as they draw nearer to Him.

Optional Activities
1. Ask several group members to research and report on the themes of Haggai, Zechariah, and Malachi.
2. Study examples of prophecy as illustrated in Zechariah. Make the following assignments: vision (5:1-4); symbolic act (6:9-15); prophetic message (7:1–8:17); oracle (14:1-21).
3. Play a recording of "By My Spirit" (Word Music) which is based on Zechariah 4:6.

Assignment
1. Review Sessions 1–12.
2. Memorize Zechariah 4:6. Review the key verses for Sessions 1–12.

REVIEW

Session Topic: God wants us to remember and apply what we've learned about Him in the prophetic books of the Old Testament. Choose one or two review methods, based on the size and interests of your group.

Option 1
Play "Stump the Panel." Ask several volunteers to participate on two panels. The remainder of the group should write questions about the Books of Isaiah through Malachi, trying to stump the panels with their questions. If one panel is unable to answer a question, the question is passed to their opponents. Keep score to make this competitive.

Option 2
Use the names and places found in each chapter to play "Wheel of Fortune" or "Probe" with your group. New group members or members who missed several sessions will be able to participate since they merely have to choose consonants to fill in the blanks on a chalkboard or poster board. Be sure to alert each team whether the words are people, places, things, or phrases.

Option 3
Review by providing group members with the opportunity to raise questions, discuss problems, or share opinions on issues that had to be omitted during the course.

Option 4
Review the key verses from each session. Provide some sort of reward or certificate for all group members who have memorized all key verses.

Option 5
Test your knowledge of the prophets by completing Prophet Trivia on page 178.

Option 6
Ask: **How has this study affected your spiritual life? How has God worked in your life during this study? What did you find most helpful? Why?** Close with prayer, asking God to help you follow the example of the Old Testament prophets by placing your confidence in Him.

Option 7
If your group members are concluding the **BibleLog Thru the Old Testament Series** with this book, make a copy of the certificate on page 161 and recognize each person who has completed Books 1–4. Then suggest that group members write the authors (c/o Victor Books, 1825 College Avenue, Wheaton, Illinois 60187) a personal note of encouragement, describing how they have grown as a result of this inductive Bible study series.

PROPHET TRIVIA

(Match the trivia with the correct prophet.)

1. Husband of a prostitute — Haggai
2. Shepherd of Tekoa — Jonah
3. Reluctant missionary — Malachi
4. The Morasthite — Daniel
5. Possible descendant of Hezekiah — Ezekiel
6. Last minor prophet — Obadiah
7. Weeping prophet — Habakkuk
8. God's watchman prophet — Zephaniah
9. Known in Babylon as Belteshazzar — Amos
10. His name means "Jehovah is God" — Hosea
11. Wrote shortest O.T. book — Micah
12. The Elkoshite — Joel
13. His name means "Yahweh is salvation" — Isaiah
14. Seer of visions, whirling wheels, and dry bones — Nahum
15. First postexilic prophet — Jeremiah
16. A contemporary of Haggai — Zechariah

Answers: (1) Hosea; (2) Amos; (3) Jonah; (4) Micah; (5) Zephaniah; (6) Malachi; (7) Jeremiah; (8) Habakkuk; (9) Daniel; (10) Joel; (11) Obadiah; (12) Nahum; (13) Isaiah; (14) Ezekiel; (15) Haggai; (16) Zechariah.

WRAP-UP

BibleLog Old Testament Book 4

Please take a minute to fill out and mail this form giving us your candid reaction to this material. Thanks for your help!

1. In what setting did you use this **BibleLog** study?

If you used Book 4 for personal study only, skip to question 7.
2. How many people were in your group?

3. What was the age range of those in your group?

4. How many weeks did you spend on this study?

5. How long was your average meeting time?

6. Did you complete the studies before discussing them with a group?

7. How long did it take you to complete the study on your own?

8. Do you plan to continue the **BibleLog** Series? Why or why not?

Would you like more information on Bible study resources for small groups?

Name _____

Address _____

Church _____

City_____State_____Zip_____

179

PLACE
STAMP
HERE

Adult Education Editor
Victor Books
1825 College Avenue
Wheaton, Illinois 60187